"I wish I had this book available to me because I am a true perfectionist. Although I've worked on my perfectionism over many years, I can see where this book would've helped me. Eleanor is a beautiful writer and she has made this so powerful with her short pages of insights. I think it would have helped me to be more of a "recovering" perfectionist. Thank you, Eleanor, for writing this important book."

–Kathy Collard Miller, Author of 62 books,
including *Managing Anger Jesus Style*

Perfectly Imperfect

101 Days to a Happier, Healthier Life
—God's Way

PERFECTLY IMPERFECT

ELEANOR KIRK

Copyright © 2025 by Eleanor Kirk

All rights reserved. No part of this publication may be reproduced, stored in a retrieval system or transmitted in any form or by any means, without express written permission of the author, except in the case of brief quotations embodied in critical reviews and certain noncommercial uses permitted by copyright law.

All scriptures cited in this book are from the New King James Version (NKJV), © 1982 Thomas Nelson. Used by permission.

For more information contact eleanorkirk@hotmail.com

Published by Elmay

ISBN (paperback): 979-8-9930784-0-3
ISBN (ebook): 979-8-9930784-1-0

Book design and production by www.AuthorSuccess.com

Printed in the United States of America

This book is dedicated to my brother, "Mr. Clean,"
who worked so hard to make his life perfect.

And to my readers, who are tired of striving for perfection and
eagerly seeking happier, healthier lifestyles. You have my deepest
respect. May God reward your journey with great success.

Download the free workbook, *Perfectly Imperfect Workbook: 101 Days to a Happier, Healthier Life—God's Way,* with section introductions and expanded questions at www.eleanorkirk.com. Watch for songs and meditations designed to debunk additional lies of the enemy. Join the Perfectly Imperfect Community on Facebook, a nurturing support group eager to hear your story. Tell us what you've learned and how the lessons have impacted your life. Share your struggles and ask your questions. You don't have to journey alone.

Disclaimers

Perfectly Imperfect: 101 Days to a Happier, Healthier Life—God's Way will work miracles for the reader who is ready to move into a more abundant life. The living Word of God, empowered by the Holy Spirit, destroys the lies of the enemy and replaces them with the truths of God's word, resulting in a great awakening of physical, mental, and spiritual powers never experienced before.

The reader who is fearful of change will be exposed to the truth and challenged to move forward. I pray the scales be removed from the eyes of each person who gazes on these words, so they may receive more than they've imagined possible. As Jesus said, "If you can believe, all things are possible to him who believes" (Mark 9:23).

Some who read this book may form a bad opinion of my mother. I mention her only to illustrate my own struggles. I adored my mother, told her she was the best mother in the world, and wanted to be just like her. She was a beautiful woman who learned to arc weld and built war planes. She worked for Lockheed before going into food service, where she moved up from waitress to chef to manager.

Unfortunately, my mother had never been nurtured. When she was little, Grandma took her to the farm where she'd been raised and left her and her little sister with a stern great aunt who had never had children. During the Great Depression, Mother had ample food but no love, cuddling, or affirmation. My aunt related that many of the things Mother said to me were the words of the great aunt who had raised them. She was trying to help me, using the only model she'd known.

I greatly admire my mother's resilience. She never abandoned her children, as her own mother had, and she worked very hard to see we had enough to eat and something to enjoy, even if it was a tumbleweed sprayed white she set up for a Christmas tree. She really was the best mother in the world.

INTRODUCTION

When a cocky student pilot on final approach touched down a little too fast, his wheels hit the runway with such force that the Cessna 150 bounded back into the air. Although he had to put her down two more times before his airspeed had fallen enough to plant the wheels firmly on the ground, he was undaunted. As he turned onto the taxiway, he radioed the tower. "Could you give me my landing time?"

"Nine-thirty-one, nine-thirty-two, and nine-thirty-three!" the controller intoned.

At least the student pilot wanted to get down. I never did. I wanted to soar up in the clouds of Never-Never Land, where everything is exactly as I would like and nothing is messy or distasteful. Of course, there were times when I smacked down so hard I thought I was glued to the runway, only to bounce back up into the ethereal realms of pretense. If you, like me, are a recovering perfectionist, you may have suffered some hard bumps as well. Life has a way of knocking us off what Mother called my "high horse."

Perfectionism is an insidious, destructive addiction, all the more difficult to shake because it's socially acceptable. Each of us probably has a touch of this drive in some area, but the addict finds the drive permeating almost everything. Until I hit bottom, I was proud of my perfectionism, equating flawlessness with excellence. I patted myself on the back for being a good little girl: the model of a self-sacrificing daughter, wife, and mother.

My wheels first slammed into the runway the year my mother brought an unruly five-year-old grandson along on her two-week visit. Within days, she was in tears, accusing me of thinking my family was perfect while looking down on everyone else. She would have gone home that day had there been an available flight! Her accusation depressed me. I was not the perfect daughter.

My wheels touched down the second time when my sixteen-year-old son was expelled from a prestigious private school toward the end of his junior year. No one would tell me why. As soon as he turned eighteen, he moved out to live with a friend. Soon after my teenage daughter turned eighteen, she chose to live in a group care home. Obviously, I was not the perfect mother.

My wheels finally fastened onto the runway when my husband of twenty-seven years bought himself an apartment and moved out. Our friends were shocked. I had been careful to maintain the illusion of a perfect marriage. Sitting alone in an empty house, I realized I was not a perfect wife, but I still hoped I was a perfect Christian. In the midst of my divorce, the good-little-girl image I'd worked so hard to preserve crashed and burned. The heavens turned to brass, and God seemed to have gone on a long journey, leaving me alone.

I turned to fasting and prayer. Head pounding, I sat at my desk and wrote, one by one, the sentences which came to me. Reading them, I discovered a progression of steps leading from the illusion in which I had lived so painfully to the reality where God dwelt. I began reading them as daily affirmations. They have changed my life, so I'm sharing them with you, praying you too will discover what I did. You are already good enough.

If you are glancing through this book, you already know perfectionism hurts. You may be the one suffering, or you may be looking for a resource to help a friend or loved one who can't seem to be satisfied with her best efforts. *Perfectly Imperfect: 101 Days to a Happier, Healthier Life—God's Way* will lead you through a successful journey out of perfectionism.

Perhaps you're unsure if you even have a problem. Perfectionism is subtle. Some catch the bug from others, such as parents, teachers, or pastors, and those deprived of unconditional love are especially susceptible. Childish logic may have persuaded you that if you could only be good enough, you could earn the love you craved.

The good news is you're already good enough. If no one has told you before, I'm sorry. I discovered this truth recently myself. Once I learned to uproot the perfectionistic tendencies eroding my well-being, life has become much less painful and infinitely more rewarding. Take this short inventory to determine if your personal hard drive is infected with the perfectionism virus.

This book may help you if:

1. You go to work when you're sick to maintain a perfect record.

2. You feel uneasy when complimented or criticized.

3. You sometimes feel like a second-class citizen.

4. You feel nervous when a situation is out of your control.

5. You have trouble making decisions.

6. You are a first-class procrastinator.

7. You think of yourself as a victim and blame others for your problems.

8. Your inner voices tend to be critical.

9. You feel responsible for the feelings or actions of others.

10. You tend to view most issues as either black or white.

11. You're not sure who you are or what you want.

12. You expect more of yourself than you do of anyone else.

13. You obsess about a critical remark for hours or even days.

14. You struggle to relax and often find leisure time stressful.

15. You analyze yourself endlessly.

If you see yourself in several of these characteristics, you may be suffering unnecessarily from distorted thinking. Following the journey mapped out in this book will help you remove the virus from the personal hard drive between your ears. This program can increase your sense of well-being, even if you have expended years or decades in a fruitless search for relief.

This practical guide will systematically confront the hidden roots of your pain and help you rebuild a healthy system of expectations. Each day is followed by a series of questions for reflection, which are great starting points for a journal or group discussion. Please, don't expect magic. Expect a miracle. Hard work is involved in replacing bad habits, but an abundant, satisfying life awaits those willing to face the truth. As Jesus said, "And you shall know the truth, and the truth shall make you free" (John 8:32).

Humble Suggestions

Reading the 101 Affirmations takes five minutes. You may choose to read them upon awakening, before bed, or not at all. There is no *best* way to use this book, only the method that works for you. If you are a writer, you may find journaling your reflections helpful. If you process your thoughts orally, you may prefer discussing them with a fellow traveler.

Anyone who has undertaken a pilgrimage toward freedom knows such journeys are beset by temptations to give up. Let's acknowledge them now. You may skip a day or even a week. You may slip back into old patterns of thinking. So what? At least you're recognizing them. Keep moving forward, one baby step at a time, and you are already victorious.

As you overwrite poisonous thinking with healthy, new ideas, you will begin to experience an exhilarating sense of liberty. You will quiet your demanding inner voice and trust God to provide His perfection. Join me in a journey out of the shadows of dark foreboding into the sunlight of bright hope.

I salute you. May your travels be crowned with great joy and overwhelming success. If you can find a small group to join you or even one fellow traveler, you will be blessed. But don't wait for a more opportune moment. Today is your day.

101 Affirmations

1. Few decisions are absolute.

2. Most choices are relative.

3. All-or-none thinking is painful.

4. I take a balanced approach to decision-making.

5. Few people get exactly what they want.

6. I am not entitled to special privileges.

7. I do not need to have everything I want.

8. I enjoy what's available.

9. I'm learning to enjoy imperfect things.

10. Happiness comes when I accept my circumstances.

11. God doesn't hate me. He loves me.

12. I am not a victim.

13. The dictator is only one of my inner voices.

14. I refuse to let the dictator bully me.

15. God is more powerful than my inner dictator.

16. God will help me refocus my life.

17. God will not magically transform me.

18. I am the person I have chosen to be.

19. I have the power to change.

20. I choose to think realistically.

21. I don't need to control everything.

22. I can't control God.

23. I refuse to control my friends and family.

24. I can control only one person—myself.

25. People resent being controlled.

26. Forcing my desires on others is a sin.

27. Things don't have to turn out the way I want.

28. God is sovereign.

29. My need to control is painful.

30. Pride resists God.

31. Pride must die before God can rule.

32. When pride is dead, the war is over.

33. I put pride to death every day.

34. My surrender must be absolute.

35. I ask God to reveal anything I'm holding back.

36. I thank God for being willing to direct my life.

37. God knows all about me, but He never gives up on me.

38. I want God to direct my life.

39. I can learn to feel safe when God's in control.

40. Trusting God is more difficult than I realized.

41. I fear God's control because I haven't tried it.

42. I trust God to take charge of my life.

43. God can do a better job of protecting me than I can.

44. I surrender my right to be in control.

45. I ask God to take over my life.

46. I relax, knowing God will provide for me.

47. God is attentive to my needs.

48. I no longer think of myself as a victim.

49. The things I feared are phantoms.

50. I release the strain of protecting myself.

51. I take shelter in God's arms.

52. I am learning to trust God's protection.

53. God's secret service surrounds me.

54. I fear only God.

55. I reject every ungodly fear.

56. Isolation is painful and unhealthy.

57. God created me to relate to others.

58. The pain of isolation is intense.

59. I choose to nurture healthy relationships.

60. God is real.

61. God is bigger than my walls.

62. God wants me to experience hope.

63. God is knocking at my door.

64. God will not demolish my defenses.

65. God will teach me to tear down my walls.

66. I release the need to be perfect.

67. It's okay to make a mistake.

68. It's okay to get sick.

69. It's okay not to know everything.

70. It's okay if someone gets angry with me.

71. It's okay if someone dislikes me.

72. It's okay if I don't measure up.

73. It's okay to feel, even to feel angry.

74. It's okay to be angry with God.

75. It's okay to release my anger.

76. It's okay to hope.

77. It's never too late to change.

78. I detect self-defeating thoughts immediately.

79. My absolute thinking is deeply ingrained.

80. Change takes time and effort.

81. I need energy, perseverance, and wisdom.

82. I ask God for everything I need.

83. I am satisfied to recover slowly or imperfectly.

84. I never give up.

85. I thank God for everything that happens.

86. I forgive all who have hurt me.

87. I ask God to forgive those who hurt me.

88. I forgive God for disappointing me.

89. I ask forgiveness for every wrong I've done.

90. I accept God's forgiveness.

91. I forgive myself.

92. I am thankful to be alive.

93. I accept God's plans for my life.

94. I am discovering who I am.

95. I am willing to be an ordinary person.

96. I overcome every obstacle.

97. I have God's peace.

98. I leave the past behind.

99. I delight in God's goodness.

100. I love who I am.

101. I confront discouraging thoughts immediately.

Day 1:
Absolute Decisions

"The way of a fool is right in his own eyes, but he who heeds counsel is wise" (Proverbs 12:15).

What makes a man a fool? According to King Solomon, the inability to consider the counsel of others makes one a simpleton. The fool sees decisions as absolute, black or white. But only a few actually are. No one was ever a little pregnant, a bit married, or half-saved. These are absolutes.

When the recently rejected officer candidate in the movie *An Officer and a Gentleman* asked the girl of his dreams to marry him, the answer was an unexpected no. He went out and hung himself. The friend who cut him down agonized, "Why didn't you talk to me?"

The dead man hadn't been able to see more than one option. Fellow travelers see possibilities we can't. I hope you'll consider me your friend as we navigate this journey together. You don't have to agree with everything I say; all I ask is for you to consider your options. There are probably more than you realize.

Perhaps you thought that if you didn't make mistakes, God would love you. Everyone else would too, and you would finally be happy. Those who believe this lie spend hours ruminating about past mistakes. *Where did I go wrong? How can I avoid repeating that error?*

**Do you want to succeed?
Abandon the drive to be perfect.**

Focusing on past errors prevents us from enjoying the present and dooms us to repeat the same mistakes. Sooner or later, we will *do* what we've been thinking. As the wise man said in Proverbs 23:7, "For as he thinks in his heart, so is he."

Start by spotting the flaw in your original premise: If I don't make mistakes, God will love me. No, God *already* loves you so much that there is nothing you could do to make Him love you more. He's already covered your past mistakes and chosen not to remember them! He's intent on giving you a rich new life, a life that will remain out of reach as long as you focus on becoming perfect. The drive for perfection forces its victim to see any deviation from the ideal as failure. In reality, your deviation from perfection may be progress. Want to succeed? Abandon the drive to be perfect.

Day 1: Questions for Reflection

1. Which absolute decisions have you handled wisely?
2. Which absolute decisions have you regretted?
3. How satisfied are you with your ability to make decisions?
4. What proportion of your decisions are absolute?
5. Which is the best decision you've made?
6. Who have you told about your worst decision?
7. How can you become more comfortable making decisions?

AFFIRMATION 1:

Few choices are absolute.

Day 2:
Relative Choices

"All things are lawful for me, but not all things are helpful; all things are lawful for me, but not all things edify." (1 Corinthians 10:23).

Imagine a hundred-point scale of acceptability. While absolute choices offer only two options, zero or one hundred, relative choices provide all the options in between, plus zero and one hundred. A person who demands flawlessness will be disappointed most of the time, for this elusive gem is rarely found by searching, earned by working, or gained by wishing. With eyes focused unblinkingly on his goal, the perfectionist deprives himself of much that could have provided satisfaction and enjoyment. Anything less than the elusive one hundred is automatically disqualified.

When my husband bought a sailboat with shabby, sunburned curtains, I was determined to sew the ideal replacements. I could see them in my mind's eye: white cotton with jaunty red and blue anchors to match the blue carpet. A visit to the local fabric store quickly took the wind out of my sails. They didn't have the fabric I wanted. Frantically, I inventoried the yardage in every store on Oahu, only to discover that there was not an inch of material with a nautical theme. Give up my impossible dream and settle for gingham? Never!

You lose out when you settle for nothing because you can't find what you want.

Perfection beckons bewitchingly, always slightly out of reach. Holding out for the ideal usually nets a big fat zero. Truth be told, there are few hundreds in the world. I sometimes suspect there are none. Things which appear perfect may simply be excellent illusions. How many people have endured heartbreaking years of loneliness waiting for the mate who meets all their criteria while surrounded by excellent choices? You lose when you settle for nothing because you can't find exactly what you want.

The malcontent has as many choices as the contented people around him. He just hasn't been able to bring himself to exercise them. Are you tired of settling for zero, tired enough to disengage from the absolute and try a few relative decisions? You *can* learn to make informed choices from the available options and enjoy the results. Who knows? I might have liked the gingham curtains.

Day 2: Questions for Reflection

1. How easily do you make decisions?
2. What proportion of your choices are relative?
3. Which of your choices turned out well?
4. Why do you prefer absolute choices or relative choices?
5. In which areas are you more absolute?
6. How has perfectionism helped you?
7. Which choice caused the most pain?

AFFIRMATION 2:

Most choices are relative.

Day 3:
Painful Thinking

"For the LORD gives wisdom; From His mouth comes knowledge and understanding." (Proverbs 2:6).

On my ninth birthday, I proudly pressed the dress I was going to wear to my party, unplugged the iron, and lifted the appliance onto a high closet shelf. Peering up at the shiny surface, I decided it was too near the edge, so I placed the palm of my hand on the hot metal to push the iron back to a safer position. From my absolute viewpoint, that iron was either plugged in and hot or unplugged and cold. Fortunately, God had designed my body to respond instantly and automatically, and my hand jerked away before I felt the burn. The throbbing blisters did put a damper on my birthday fun, but they soon healed. The pain inflicted by absolute thinking took much longer.

When I was limited by absolute thinking, I lived in an excruciating, destructive loop. I stood at the zero mark, looking up at the one hundred mark high above, my impossible dream. I leaped, exerting every ounce of strength, seeing that height as the only alternative to the slimy pit in which my feet were mired. Upward I soared: fifty, sixty, seventy, seventy-five. Oh no! I began to lose momentum with the goal still out of reach. Defeated for the umpteenth time, I flopped back to zero. The splat into the slimy pit left me dazed but undaunted. I pasted a grim smile on my face and tried again, and again, and *again*. Eventually, the slime felt like home. Life was managing bruises. Hope was a cruel joke.

You really can choose to enjoy what's available.

As surely as God designed a system of safeguards for the body, He also installed an alarm for the mind, but you may be afraid of that warning signal. You may have chosen to deny, disarm, and repress the anger God meant to energize you to resolve your problems. Instead of cursing the destructive, absolute standards that weigh you down, have you felt cursed because you failed to achieve them?

In place of enjoying the abundant life Jesus suffered to provide, you, like me, may have insisted on doing your own suffering. Let's make a change today. The next time you jump for the one-hundred mark, grasp the highest ledge you can reach and hold on. You may only attain a fifty, but a fifty is a lot better than a nosedive into the slime. Besides, the next time you jump, you can start from the fifty-foot ledge and get a lot closer to the top. The choice has been yours all along. You really *can* choose to enjoy what's available.

Day 3: Questions for Reflection

1. Why did you begin to strive for perfection?
2. Who or what encouraged you to be perfect?
3. How much pain has absolute thinking caused?
4. What did you do with your pain?
5. Which areas of your life suffer the most?
6. How have you used your anger?
7. What would change if you stopped striving?

AFFIRMATION 3:

All-or-none thinking is painful.

Day 4:
Balanced Thinking

"Therefore, do not worry, saying, 'What shall we eat?' or 'What shall we drink?' or 'What shall we wear?' For after all these things the Gentiles seek. For your heavenly Father knows that you need all these things. But seek first the kingdom of God and His righteousness, and all these things shall be added to you" (Matthew 6:31-33).

Magic fascinates young and old alike. Abracadabra! A white bunny disappears into thin air, or a beautiful girl appears out of nowhere. What fun! I wonder what magic you would like to perform in your life? Maybe you'd like to say, "Poof!" and be instantly rich or beautiful, or "Open sesame!" and be accepted into the popular group, or have everyone in your family love you. Many of us would like to transform our less-than-perfect lives into a fairy tale.

I waited for my fairy godmother to transform me into a princess and for Prince Charming to carry me off to his castle, where I could live happily ever after. I waited in vain. My prince must have taken a wrong turn because he never showed up. Neither did my fairy godmother, and I really needed her. I'd fallen under the spell of an evil witch named Magical Thinking.

Fairy tales are absolute. The bad guys are all bad. (We don't defend the witch because she had a bad childhood. She's bad—all bad, and we're relieved when she dies.) The good guys are all good. (You don't worry about your fairy godmother gossiping about you. She is goodness personified, and you rejoice when she triumphs.) In a fairy tale, everything is black or white. Life is absolutely miserable before the magic moment and perfectly wonderful afterward.

Once you stop waiting for Prince Charming, you're free to enjoy the life God gave you.

Have you noticed that real life doesn't work that way? Your best moments are often tainted with something disagreeable, perhaps as small as a pit in your cherry pie, hard enough to crack a tooth. Your worst moments may sport a tiny blessing, as in the radiant smile on your toddler's face as she proudly shows you the mural she crayoned on her bedroom wall.

As you bumble through life, attempting to choose the good and refuse the evil, your options seem to be a mixture of the two. Slogging through an ordinary day, you find yourself sorting through possibilities that are neither breathtaking nor horrifying. Have you ever owned a ball gown worthy of glass slippers? I haven't. My closet is full of ordinary clothes, well-suited to my ordinary life. Once I stopped waiting for Prince Charming to round the corner on his white charger, I was free to enjoy them.

Day 4: Questions for Reflection

1. What is the difference between *good* and *perfect*?
2. How has *magical thinking* affected you?
3. What magical moments have you experienced?
4. What wishes would you like to see come true?
5. How do you feel about your everyday life?
6. Do you know anyone who's lived "happily ever after?"
7. Which relative choices sometimes seem like absolutes?

AFFIRMATION 4:

I take a balanced approach to decision-making.

Day 5:
Accepting Second Best

"Do not fret because of evildoers, nor be envious of the workers of iniquity. For they shall soon be cut down like the grass, And wither as the green herb" (Psalms 37:1-2).

Everywhere you look, you see people enjoying the very things you imagine would make *you* happy. Ah, but do they bring *them* happiness? That's the question. One day, a woman who exercises at my fitness club showed up with a new hairdo. I couldn't take my eyes off her. A formerly drab individual had been transformed into a radiant beauty. When I ventured to compliment her on her new look, she unleashed a diatribe against the stylist who had *dared* to cut her hair shorter than she'd instructed. Amazing!

The gorgeous woman had no idea how wonderful she looked! So great was her fury that later in the same week, she cut her hair very short. The next time I saw her, she was back to drab. Have you, like her, found yourself powerless to enjoy an unexpected blessing that didn't conform to your desires?

You may spend a great deal of time trying to get exactly what you want, only to discover the coveted item or experience fails to provide the pleasure you had anticipated. Life is tricky that way. Contentment is the fruit of accepting and enjoying what God gives, which is easier when you stop scrutinizing His gifts for defects. Those pesky flaws are always present, but they don't have to spoil your enjoyment.

The Bible tells the fantastic story of Solomon, the man who was in a position to acquire everything his heart desired. He was the richest, wisest, and most miserable creature on Earth. How do I know? He tells us as much in the first chapter of Ecclesiastes. "All things are full of labor; Man cannot express it. The eye is not satisfied with seeing, nor the ear filled with hearing. I have seen all the works that are done under the sun; and, indeed, all is vanity and grasping for the wind" (Ecclesiastes 1:8,14).

Contentment is the fruit of accepting and enjoying what God provides.

A man who had a thousand women dedicated to his pleasure penned those words! He had satisfied every desire of his heart to the utmost: written books, planted orchards, made alliances, and built an awesome temple, as well as a palace. One thing eluded him: contentment.

If you're skeptical, do your own research. Ask your family, coworkers, church members, and carpool riders, "Do you have exactly what you want?"

My guess is you'll find contentment in short supply. Maybe our medicine cabinets are so well stocked with pain relievers and antacids because we have difficulty accepting the fact that almost no one gets *exactly* what they want. Do you?

Day 5: Questions for Reflection

1. What exactly do you want?
2. How would your life be different if you had every-thing you wanted?
3. Would this change be positive or negative?
4. What flaws do you expect to discover in the object of your desire?
5. Which flaws will compromise your enjoyment?
6. What would make you feel better about the flaws?
7. Do you know anyone who has everything he wants? Is he happy?

AFFIRMATION 5:

Few people get exactly what they want.

Day 6:
The Quest to Be Special

"For I say, through the grace given to me, to everyone who is among you, not to think of himself more highly than he ought to think, but to think soberly, as God has dealt to each one a measure of faith" (Romans 12:3).

Many squander the energy of youth on a quest to be special. Perhaps you were among them. Did you think you had to be outstanding as well as unique? Did you labor under the notion that you could earn the approval of others by scrambling to the top of the heap? Surely then you would be noticed and appreciated. You may have climbed over many who *were* noticed and appreciated despite being at the bottom of the heap. Perhaps you, like me, failed to realize that people are attracted to those who admit their flaws, rather than those who flaunt their perfection.

Homecoming is a huge event in high school football, and little compares to the honor of being crowned homecoming king. I was not present that moonlit evening when an act of selfless generosity changed two lives, but I heard the story afterward. Let's reconstruct the scene. Though the details may be blurry, similar scenarios have played out in numerous schools across the nation.

As the students of Sedona Red Rock High School watched, thrones were set out on the recently-installed artificial turf. Teenagers rose to their feet and cheered as the king, a tall, handsome athlete, was crowned, but then the cheer crescendoed into a roar as the newly crowned star placed his trophy on the head of Pete, the senior with Down syndrome, neither tall, nor handsome, nor athletic. Everyone loved Pete. Why? Perhaps because he always sported a comical grin and never competed with anyone. He had made it his mission to love everyone. That night, Pete was noticed and more than noticed. Pete was celebrated. Have you felt the approval that washed over him that night as he pushed the crown out of his eyes?

People are attracted to those who admit their flaws, rather than those who flaunt their perfection.

Many children who failed to win their mother's or father's approval focus their energies on winning God's. Is He impressed with their efforts? Would He accept them if they kept His commandments more stringently? Performed extra Christian service? Deprived themselves of enough pleasure? They don't know the answers to these questions. They only know that they never feel embraced. Never feel loved. Sadly, the love they are desperately seeking eludes them. They cannot attain love by perfecting themselves.

My determination to be special only made me different, and people are rarely attracted to those they perceive as different. I believed hard work could earn the love of God and man. Did you, like me, never feel special but never stop trying? Did you see each new venture as another opportunity to distinguish yourself? Did you think you needed to be superior to be loved? I wish I had known that God already loved me! He already loves you, too. You don't have to qualify for God's love because Jesus met all the qualifications for you. You're already accepted.

The Apostle Paul asks a great question. "For who makes you differ from another? And what do you have that you did not receive? Now if you did indeed receive it, why do you boast as if you had not received it" (1 Cor. 4:7)?

Why indeed!

Day 6: Questions for Reflection

1. What does it mean to *you* to be special?
2. Why do you want to be better than others?
3. How have you striven to distinguish yourself?
4. Who is your favorite person?
5. What makes this person special?
6. Are you comfortable with who you are?
7. What does God expect of you?

AFFIRMATION 6:

I am not entitled to special privileges.

Day 7:
Content in Disappointment

"Not that I speak in regard to need, for I have learned in whatever state I am, to be content" (Philippians 4:11).

A mother pushing her cart through the aisle of a supermarket, toddler in tow, paused to read the label on a cereal box. Her little one spied a brightly-colored carton at his eye level. He didn't need to read anything. He *knew* what he wanted.

"Buy Count Chocula, Mommy!" he demanded, clutching the prize in his chubby arms.

"Not this time, sweetheart." She reached for the contraband. "Mommy's not getting that one."

You know the rest of the story. You've watched her wrestle the battered box from her child. You've covered your ears as she picked up the boy, plopped him into the shopping cart, and disappeared around the corner. As the curtain fell on the little drama and the ear-splitting wails faded, you may have smirked at the display of childish immaturity. I did.

Oops! God suddenly reminded me of how often I've played the toddler in my interactions with Him. I know exactly *what* I want and *when* I want it. *Now! Thank you very much.* I am obsessed with my happiness and the multitude of little details I'm sure would guarantee it. God has His own agenda. He's more interested in holiness than happiness, and He's willing to mop up a bathtub of tears and endure some deafening wails to achieve His goal.

Can you say, "God, I'm really upset about this!" when things don't go your way?

Have you thanked God that you haven't always gotten what you wanted? Where would you be if you had? Your heavenly Father is too wise and loving to be overruled by any temper fit. He plays the parent role well. Do you do justice to the toddler part? That little guy was authentic in expressing his outrage. Adults rarely manage that degree of openness. Instead of confessing I'm angry with God, I may mope, get depressed, or feel worthless. Have you tried my tactic of attempting to get even with God by punishing yourself? *Maybe when He sees how miserable I am, He'll be sorry He didn't give me what I wanted.* If so, maybe you want to join me in saying, "God, I'm really upset about this!" the next time things don't go your way.

Day 7: Questions for Reflection

1. How did you handle a childhood disappointment?
2. Who did you tell about your problem?
3. How does your disappointment still affect you?
4. Have you told God what happened?
5. How do you feel when God says no?
6. Rate your patience on a scale of one to ten.
7. Can you be content with what's available?

AFFIRMATION 7:

I do not have to have what I want.

"I know how to be abased, and I know how to abound. Everywhere and in all things I have learned both to be full and to be hungry, both to abound and to suffer need" (Phil. 4:12).

Like many in low-income families, I grew up eating the most economical meat. The main course was sautéed in spaghetti sauce, rolled up in cabbage leaves, and baked into meatloaves. My mother could have written *101 Ways to Cook Hamburger*. I enjoyed those meals. She never mentioned we were eating the cheapest meat because we couldn't afford the more expensive cuts, and I never figured out she earned fifty cents an hour serving sirloin steak to her customers so her family could eat ground beef. In retrospect, I realize our experience of those humble meals was quite different. I enjoyed them; she wished for something better. Contentment is a great condiment. What a pity my mother missed out on the everyday goodness of hamburger meat.

I wonder what you've missed. When you couldn't have *exactly* what you wanted, did you get disgusted and do without? My family of origin included an abusive stepfather, a mother who thought me hopelessly bereft of common sense, a brother who was sure I was crazy, and a sister who married an alcoholic. When I moved to

Hawaii, I discovered that 2,000 miles of water provided a formidable buffer. I could raise my children free of the chaos of my family of origin. I was finally alone—and incredibly lonely. Who knows what I missed? I'm sure you were wiser.

Can you enjoy what God's provided rather than depriving yourself?

Like me, you may have taken years to realize that God hasn't offered you a choice of family, only an option of whether or not to enjoy the one He's provided. When you fail to embrace them, everyone suffers. This is true of more than families, so I've settled on a new course of action. I'm no longer going to deprive myself every time my ideal isn't accessible. I'm going to enjoy what's available. What about you? Can you enjoy what God's provided rather than depriving yourself?

Day 8: Questions for Reflection

1. What is your biggest need?
2. How would you prefer to have your need supplied?
3. What options are available?
4. How are you using the resources you have?
5. When will you enjoy what God's provided?
6. What are you tolerating that you could be enjoying?
7. What do you have that's second best—but treasured?

AFFIRMATION 8:

I enjoy what's available.

Day 9: Appreciating Imperfection

"So why do you worry about clothing? Consider the lilies of the field, how they grow: they neither toil nor spin; and yet I say to you that even Solomon in all his glory was not arrayed like one of these" (Matt. 6:28-29).

One glance at the price tag dangling from the sleeve of the dress informed me the garment was out of my price range, but another tag hanging below the first caught my eye. "Any imperfections you may notice in this material are not manufacturing defects. They are called 'slubs.' They result from using natural fibers and are to be considered an integral part of the beauty of the fabric."

Whoa! Wait a minute. That little piece of information was worth more than a dozen expensive dresses. "Slub" was more than a new word. Slub was a whole new concept. If a soft, thick, uneven section in a yarn or thread could *add* to its beauty instead of spoil it, I had been looking at things all wrong. Do you, like me, find yourself observing life through distorted glasses?

Perfection was a highly valued concept in school. Everyone wanted a paper marked 100 percent or a big red "A+" pinned on the bulletin board for the others to admire and emulate. Didn't you try to color inside the lines and write your letters *exactly* like the model taped above the blackboard? Perfection was the price of recognition, and perfection was, if not uniformity, at least conformity. All the papers on the board looked the same. I can assure you they had no "slubs" in them; no soft, uneven spots. No indeed.

You can learn to accept, appreciate, and even enjoy the irregular beauty around you.

"Manufacture" originally meant to make by hand, so each item necessarily displayed the uniqueness of the human hand that had created it. With the introduction of machinery, man could, for the first time, produce a uniform, *perfect* product. Dreary uniformity became the norm and eventually the standard of beauty. Flaws were no longer acceptable. Man, who had created the machine, was duped into admiring and emulating his invention and, in the process, lost his appreciation of the natural and the imperfect.

As perfect as a silk rose may appear, you're disappointed when you realize it's artificial. A real blossom may be less symmetrical, but the genuine flower exudes the sweet fragrance of life. As you make your way through this imperfect world, you can learn to accept, appreciate, and even enjoy the wonders of the irregular beauty around you. Learn to say, "So what." So what if a bug chewed a hole in one rose petal? The blossom is still beautiful.

Day 9: Questions for Reflection

1. How would your life be better if everything were perfect?
2. Which irregularities most disappoint you?
3. What beauty can you see in *slubs*?
4. Do you expect more of yourself or others?
5. How could you become more accepting?
6. Which flaw could you accept today?
7. What would happen if you embraced flaws?

AFFIRMATION 9:

I'm learning to enjoy imperfect things.

Day 10:
Accepting Circumstances

"Do all things without complaining and disputing, that you may become blameless and harmless, children of God without fault in the midst of a crooked and perverse generation, among whom you shine as lights in the world" (Phil. 2:14-15).

Lost en route to London, a merchant stopped to ask directions from a pig farmer. (Wait. Do men ever ask directions?) The farmer answered, "If *I* were going to London, I certainly wouldn't start here."

That's good for a laugh, but what choice did the poor bloke have?

Precisely the predicament in which you and I occasionally find ourselves! No one has any hope of arriving at his desired destination until he's willing to admit he's lost. Are you anxious to demonstrate that you *know* what you're doing? Do you *pretend* you're on your way to London when you know you've missed the turn? When your disorientation becomes obvious, do you act as though you didn't really *want* to go to London? Can you admit you're lost in Hogs' Wallow with no gas, no map, and no idea what to do next?

Playing make-believe used to be fun. As a child, you used your imagination to run toward life. You were excited to rehearse for the next stage by trying on different roles to see which ones were more fulfilling. Now you're grown up, and you may find yourself using the same marvelous faculty to run away from life and deceive yourself about where you are and who you'd like to be.

You're unhappy when you decide to dislike the situation in which the Lord has placed you.

You're unhappy when you decide to dislike the situation in which the Lord has placed you, convincing yourself you are being unjustly deprived of a more pleasant setting. Like the poor fellow lost on the way to London, you'll never get an inch closer to your goal until you admit you've made a mistake and ask for help. Seeking help can be humbling, and changing direction can be challenging. But telling the truth will be brave, noble, and a bit adventurous, and you could probably use a dash of adventure about now.

Day 10: Questions for Reflection

1. What brings you happiness?
2. How is your life's goal related to your happiness?
3. Which attitudes have gotten you closer to your goal?
4. What is unacceptable about your circumstances?
5. Which lessons can you learn from your current situation?
6. Where would you like to be five years from now?
7. How do you plan to get there?

AFFIRMATION 10:

Happiness comes when I accept my circumstances.

Day 11:
God Loves Me

"The Lord has appeared of old to me, saying:
Yes, I have loved you with an everlasting love;
Therefore with lovingkindness I have drawn you"
(Jeremiah 31:3).

Did you ever have the feeling you had gotten the short end of the stick? Did you imagine other people, be they siblings, classmates, or coworkers, had been endowed with blessings you did not receive? They possessed talents, skills, or resources that you admired and coveted but could never hope to attain. An extremely coordinated sibling was the star athlete at whatever sport they attempted, while you were born with two left feet. Or everyone else in your class grasped the new math concept, which boggled your mind. Or the girl in front of you was the most gorgeous creature you had ever laid eyes on, which left you feeling uglier than a cockroach. We've all been there. Remember the joke we cracked when we felt insecure, "When they were passing out brains, I thought they said, 'trains' and got in the wrong line."

By the time I was five, I knew God played favorites. Why else had my brother been born with silky, platinum-blond hair and sky-blue eyes, which gave him an air of angelic innocence? My dark brown hair was so dry and porous that my ponytail stuck out like a shock of wheat. My classmates tossed ponytails, which were cascades of sleek waves. I had a haystack of split ends. No amount of hot oil and steamy towels could tame my mane. I was cursed! Or so I thought. Now that I take thyroid medication, the most frequent comment I hear is, "I love your hair."

I love my hair too. It's God's gift to me.

Then there was the fact that my brother was allowed to do a lot of things I wasn't. "You're a girl," my mother would say, ending all discussion.

So while my brother was out fishing and swimming in the Florida lakes, I was home sweeping and mopping floors, ironing clothes, and cooking supper. Mother wasn't the only one who made such distinctions. Years later, when my husband and I taught at a mission school on the Mexican border, he received 50 percent more pay than I did because he was "head-of-house."

Society has changed since those days, but I didn't have to wait for those changes to discover that God didn't hate me. I only had to wait until my first child was two. I was explaining to Ricky that my big tummy meant he would soon be a brother.

He eyed me quizzically, then patted his flat midsection and announced, "When I grow up, I'm going to have a baby in *my* tummy."

You are God's child.
He has bestowed His love on you.

Uh-oh! I tried to put a positive spin on it. "Someday you can be a daddy, but because you're a boy, you can never be a mommy."

His lip shot out. No explanation was going to help. How privileged I was! I wouldn't have traded my children for fishing, swimming in the lakes, or any additional salary. God had given me a precious gift in my womanhood. I hadn't been cursed, simply self-deceived. "Behold, what manner of love the Father has bestowed on us, that we should be called children of God" (1 John 3:1).

Is anything better than that?

You are God's child. He has bestowed His love on you. As long as you remember this amazing fact and stop comparing yourself with others, you're in excellent shape. "For we dare not class ourselves or compare ourselves with those that commend themselves. But they, measuring themselves by themselves, and comparing themselves among themselves, are not wise" (2 Cor. 10:12).

Our Lord's half-brother James apparently considered the Savior to be little more than a lunatic until Jesus died. The resurrection opened James's eyes. His homeless, vagabond brother was the Lord of glory. After he met the risen Christ, James went from being an unbeliever to becoming the head of the Jerusalem church. Until you have a similar awakening and begin to see yourself and those about you with spiritual eyes, you're bound to be confused, especially because God often wraps his most outstanding gifts in plain brown paper.

Day 11: Questions for Reflection

1. With whom have you compared yourself?
2. How did the comparison make you feel?
3. What does this person have that you don't have?
4. What do you have that this person doesn't?
5. Why did God forbid comparing ourselves with others?
6. Who gave you the qualities you dislike in yourself?
7. Under what conditions could you appreciate yourself?

AFFIRMATION 11:

God doesn't hate me. He loves me.

Day 12:
Victim Mentality

"In this you greatly rejoice, though now... You have been grieved by various trials, that the genuineness of your faith, being much more precious than gold that perishes, though it is tested by fire, may be found to praise, honor, and glory at the revelation of Jesus Christ" (1 Peter 1:6-7).

Why is the temptation to self-pity so inviting? A martyr complex in others repels us. You and I are sure *we* would never choose to wallow in the stinky pit of self-pity! *Or would we?* Like a woman whose slip is showing or a man whose fly is unzipped, you and I may remain blissfully ignorant of an embarrassing fact obvious to everyone else. The person nourishing a grievance is too busy sipping the sweet nectar of "righteous indignation," alias "wounded pride," to realize the heady elixir has gone rancid. Like Eve, he poisons himself.

When I moved to Hawaii, I discovered that the friendly, laid-back atmosphere of the islands was hiding serious social unrest. On a small rock where one culture's pet is another culture's dinner, some friction was to be expected, but the chafing of cultural differences was nothing compared to the fomenting bitterness some Hawaiians harbored toward the "haoles," those they considered foreigners. They lamented the fact that chiefs of old had given tracts of land to missionaries and other new arrivals, dooming the natives to a life of poverty in paradise. Apparently, there had been no land ownership under the monarchy, unless the king owned the land. Each man lived on a "kuliana," a strip of land that ran from the ocean to the mountain, providing both fish and farmland.

While those of Hawaiian descent nursed their grievances, the Japanese were imported to work the sugar cane fields. Their story seems equally sad. They flocked to the island "for a few years" to make their fortunes and return home with comfortable nest eggs, only to discover their seemingly ample wages barely covered the cost of living. Instead of becoming bitter when they realized they would *never* be able to purchase a return ticket, they sent for "picture brides" from Japan. Within two generations, the hard-working Japanese had climbed into the upper echelons of island society. Instead of succumbing to the tantalizing temptation to indulge in a well-deserved pity party, they went to work.

When I left the islands, many native Hawaiians were still under-privileged and looking for a handout, while not so secretly fomenting a move for "sovereignty." Focused on the past, they wanted to turn the clock backward! The energy they expended bemoaning what *might have been* or waiting for what *might someday be* would have been better spent taking advantage of their amazing educational opportunities. A change of attitude could have brought a promising future.

I can either contemplate my scars and remain stuck, or I can forget the past and move forward.

I didn't see that I had made the same mistakes! I wonder if you have, too? I made excuses for my shortcomings instead of overcoming them. I begged off confronting my challenges because of a raw deal in the past. So what if my father was an alcoholic? So what if I'd moved from one coast to the other so often that I rarely finished the school year where I'd begun it? So what if my mom called me do-less? That's over, and I, like the native Hawaiians, have a choice. I can either contemplate my scars and remain stuck, or I can forget the past and move forward. What about you? Have you allowed the past to bog you down? Are you still nursing the emotional wounds of yesteryear? If so, now is your chance to step out of your pity party into the amazing possibilities available today.

Day 12: Questions for Reflection

1. When have you felt like a victim?
2. What dreams were snatched away?
3. How could you recapture those dreams?
4. Which past traumas influence you today?
5. How would you have liked your life to be different?
6. When will you make peace with your past?
7. How has your past made you stronger?

AFFIRMATION 12:

I am not a victim.

Day 13:
Inner Voices

"Your ears shall hear a word behind you, saying,
'This is the way, walk in it.' Whenever you turn to
the right hand, or whenever you turn to the left"
(Isaiah 30:21).

Have you laughed at the cartoon of the man with an angel on one shoulder whispering into one ear while a devil on the other side whispers into the other ear? You identify with the quandary of hearing more than one voice because you yourself struggle with sorting out those voices every time you're faced with a decision. But what if there are *more* than two voices, and some of them are coming from *inside* your head?

My psychologist explained that a minimum of three inner voices were competing for my attention. Stunned into submission by the piercing shout of a commanding officer, I'd rarely detected the calm voice of reason. Having abdicated control to a bully, I had allowed myself to be pushed into snap decisions not in my best interest. Yet they felt correct. The keyword here is "absolute." The inner dictator is certain about everything. When there seems to be only one way out of a dilemma, her uncompromising voice is the one we're hearing. So, what about those other two?

Your mind is a bit like a teeter-totter: two opposing forces balanced by a fulcrum. On one side is the subjective or emotional part, on the other, the objective or rational part. Since God didn't intend either of these to rule, He gave you a will, the fulcrum of your tee-ter-totter. Your volition is supposed to listen to the evidence from both sides and make a balanced decision. Whew! You don't have to obey the ranting bully. You can call a time-out, sit down with a nice cup of tea, and mull the whole thing over. You can even put the decision off for a week or a month if you need to do further research. How liberating! You don't have to be ruled by fear.

A friend used to put things in perspective by asking, "What's the worst thing that could happen?"

Her question exposed the ridiculousness of numberless fears. When my job teaching college classes started a week after bladder surgery, the doctor said I would have to wear a catheter with a bag strapped to my leg for the first few days of teaching. No way!

My friend demanded I tell her the worst thing that could happen, and we both broke out laughing. The bag could burst! So what? A moment's embarrassment was hardly worth forfeiting the position I coveted. Once I'd confronted my fear, the problem evaporated, leaving me free to recuperate, and the catheter was removed days before the semester started. Reason had prevailed over fear, and I enjoyed teaching for seven more years at that junior college.

What does your teeter-totter look like today? Have you crashed to the ground on the side of emotion, or have you called on your will to balance those runaway emotions with calm reason? You can choose to listen to your voices, mull over their input, and make wise decisions that free you to become the person God designed you to be.

You don't have to obey the ranting bully.

Day 13: Questions for Reflection

1. Which is your loudest inner voice?
3. How often are you driven to make immediate decisions?
4. How many other voices do you hear?
5. What would happen if you researched your choices?
6. Which fear drives you the hardest?
7. What is the worst thing that could happen if you faced your fear?

AFFIRMATION 13:

The dictator is only one of my inner voices.

Day 14:
The Dictator

"For I delight in the law of God according to my inward man. But I see another law in my members, warring against the law of my mind, and bringing me into captivity to the law of sin which is in my members" (Rom. 7:22-23).

Why on Earth did I do that? If you're like me, you've often asked yourself that question. There are bizarre moments when you do things you can't understand. In individuals with mental illness, the reason may be hearing voices. Now that's scary. I once took a Spanish Bible to a man who claimed a long-dead doctor had ordered him to kill two brothers in the Waikiki Burger King. That unfortunate soul is in a maximum-security prison for life.

In reality, I believe you and I both hear voices, demanding voices which may have sentenced you, as they did me, to long, dreary years in maximum-security. You experience the guidance of God, the threats of the enemy, that fallen angel also known as Satan, the counsel of reason, the clamors of emotion, the wisdom of conscience, and the demands of the inner dictator, to name a few. You haven't heard of the inner dictator? Let me introduce you to the one who controls much of your life.

A not-so-subtle force is at work deep inside your psyche. In adolescence, I thought this inner guidance was a replay of my mother's admonitions, stored in some enormous library. Every time I made a mistake, the appropriate recording played back with her exact intonations. Twenty years later, I realized I had internalized her persona. Like a well-designed computer virus, the invader had taken on a life of its own, replicating itself in a dozen different arenas. When I least expected it, a voice would boom over my private intercom. "First we *work*, and *then* we play!"

I wonder if you, too, have been mistaking the dictator for your conscience. After several years of therapy, I marvel at how gullible I was. Your bossy potentate is actually a synthesis of every critical force to which you've been exposed, starting with your parents and ending with you. When you consider the inner dictator, your bosom buddy and faithful guardian, you place a deadly arsenal at her disposal: the password to your heart, plus unlimited access to your thoughts and emotions. If you are to regain control, you must revoke the power you've given away.

Your salvation does not depend on whether you finish the housecleaning immediately.

Begin by considering the source. Once you realize the voice ordering you around is *not* your conscience, the commands lose their urgency. Your salvation does not depend on whether you finish the housecleaning immediately. Since Jesus commended Mary for sitting at his feet when her sister wanted her to work in the kitchen, I imagine He smiles when you question a drive to busyness.

"For thus says the Lord GOD, the Holy One of Israel: 'In returning and rest you shall be saved; In quietness and confidence shall be your strength'" (Isa. 30:15).

Hard work and busyness don't bring God's strength. Rest and quietness do. Mary rested at Jesus's feet while Martha busied herself in the kitchen. Imagine the courage required to sit quietly when so much needed to be done. Mary had to face down her own inner voices as well as her sister's demands. In my opinion, Mary is a heroine. You, too, can choose God's best and become the hero or heroine of your own story. But first, you'll have to confront your inner dictator.

Day 14: Questions for Reflection

1. What are you driven to do that doesn't make sense?
2. Which inner voices demand obedience?
3. Are these voices friendly? Scolding? Dictatorial?
4. What happens if you don't obey them?
5. How free are you to make your own decisions?
6. Who is your inner dictator?
7. How can you weaken the dictator's control?

AFFIRMATION 14:

I refuse to let the dictator bully me.

Day 15: Intimidation

"You shall fear the LORD your God and serve Him, and take oaths in His name" (Deuteronomy 6:13).

"For it is written, 'You shall worship the LORD your God, and Him only you shall serve'" (Luke 4:8).

Jesus modified Moses's admonition to fear and serve only God by replacing the word "fear" with "worship." Worship means to ascribe greatness and worth to something or someone. You and I instinctively fear what's greater and more powerful. Notice the disciples' reaction each time they caught a glimpse of Jesus's divinity. After the great catch of fish, Peter fell to his knees and begged Jesus to leave him because he was a sinner. The disciples were more terrified of Jesus *after* He calmed the storm than they had been of dying in the storm. All of mankind fears power.

Moses admonished Israel to fear only God. Why? You automatically serve your greatest fear, and your service requires a great deal of energy. Imagine, for instance, the work required to be afraid of dogs. You would have to avoid the homes of friends with dogs, as well as parks, streets, and even some stores. Serving fear is hard work. That's why God wants to free you from every *other* fear by fearing Him alone.

You always serve your greatest fear.

As a Christian, you know the eternal God who created the universe and guides the planets is more powerful than anything else you might fear. Yet when your inner voice intimidates you, do you cower into submission, forgetting your Father? He has promised to send His angels to encamp around those who fear Him and deliver them.

Did you notice that only those who "fear Him" are protected? Fear anything else, and you are fair game for the enemy. How vital, then, to allow only one fear, a healthy fear of God! God admonishes us, "Fear not!" over 100 times in the Bible, so why *do* we fear? If your primary goal in life is staying alive, you will fear death, the ultimate enemy.

God's still in charge. He has been from eternity past, and He will be throughout eternity future, which means you can place the car accident in front of your house in His hands as well as the nuclear accident half a world away. He's on top of it. God never sleeps, and His tender care never fails. He's there for the victims of the nuclear disaster, as surely as He's here for you.

When we moved from Ohio to Florida, I enrolled in fifth grade, a definite outsider. How could my classmates tell? For one thing, I was wearing a sweater in the tropics. For another, I greeted them with "Hi," while they all said, "Hey." I hadn't studied the Civil War yet, so I didn't understand their hostility.

At recess, my classmates called me Yankee. Some threw rocks. One rock hit me on the cheek. I felt doomed. But was I? What if I had been able to zoom out into the Spirit realm and see my Shepherd standing over me with His rod and staff, ready to defend me? He was there for me that day, even though I couldn't perceive Him. I suffered little harm. You can be sure He's there for you also.

Why doesn't the God who thundered the law from Sinai drown the voice of fear? You've chosen to tune your inner radio to the Fear Channel. You *enjoy* listening to the "fake news" spewed out by your intimidating voices. By some strange paradox, being scared makes you feel safer. You choose to be fearful rather than faithful.

When you look *around* you at the world, you find numberless reasons for fear. Thank God He gives you the privilege of looking *up* and choosing faith over fear. The next time an alarm goes off in your head, tell yourself God is with you. Then remember that He's bigger than any voice in your mind. Who's your daddy?

Day 15: Questions for Reflection

1. How much control have you given to fear?
2. Name and describe your inner voices.
3. List several of your common fears.
4. Which one feeds the others?
5. How do you see Jesus relating to your anxiety?
6. What would diminish those fears?
7. How long do you want to hold on to your anxiety?

AFFIRMATION 15:

God is more powerful than my inner dictator.

Day 16:
Asking for Help

"Bear one another's burdens, and so fulfill
the law of Christ" (Galatians 6:2).

Do you look to others when life hands you an overwhelming task? Or would you rather rely on your own resources, even when you know they're woefully inadequate? I suspect the average person asks for help only a fraction of the times they need support. For years, I blamed this reticence on my timidity, but timidity wasn't the problem. I was too proud to admit I needed help.

Pride! There's the problem. We'd all like to take pride in something we did *all by ourselves*, and asking for assistance robs us of bragging rights. In cultures that value group interaction, a person would take joy in being part of the collective that accomplished a task. Not so in the Western world. The question to ask yourself is how much you want to achieve in this life. You'll get a lot more done if you accept the expertise and strength of those about you.

By the time I was nine, I was expected to sweep, mop, dust, cook, and iron for four people with no instruction on how to perform these chores. Scoldings when I failed to measure up did nothing to improve my performance. Fortunately, my stepfather showed me how to manage the mangle, which ironed our sheets, and the flat iron for shirts, dresses, and pants, which we hung to dry on pants' stretchers. Our cotton clothing had to be washed, starched, hung to dry, sprinkled with water, and rolled up *before* being ironed.

Anything I didn't finish that day had to be stored in the refrigerator to avoid mildew.

Have you ever thought that you should have been born knowing everything? No one is fully programmed at birth, and the sooner you admit your ignorance, the happier and more productive you'll be. Progress comes in giving yourself permission *not* to know everything. Have you made peace with the fact that you are neither Superman nor Wonder Woman? Ordinary people don't know things by magic. They have to learn them, and sometimes they have to ask for help. That's okay. Get comfortable asking for help, but keep one thing in mind: others can't solve *all* your problems. Sometimes, only God has the resources you need.

The superhuman challenge you're facing right now may be the challenge of regaining control of your thought life. You may be driven by hypercritical inner voices robbing you of love, joy, and peace. If you're tired of feeling guilty about asking others for help, ask God. He not only has the power to help you, but He delights in those who call upon Him. God won't barge into your conundrum and start cleaning things up without an invitation. He waits to be asked.

For years, I was too proud to ask. I wanted to clean up my *own* mess and *then* invite Him over to compliment me on my work. How foolish! I'll never have a life worth living without Him, so I've learned to ask Him to help me every day, long before I come to the end of my resources. What about you? Have you let pride hold you back? If you see the foolishness of trying to do life on your own, say, "Lord, please help me." He'll be there before you finish speaking.

God won't barge into your conundrum and start cleaning things up without an invitation.

Day 16: Questions for Reflection

1. Which of your thoughts seems harmful?
2. What would you most like to change?
3. Which forces control your thoughts?
4. What happens if *you* try to control your thoughts?
5. How often do you ask for help?
6. Whose help would you most like to have?
7. When did you last ask God for assistance?

AFFIRMATION 16:

God will help me refocus my life.

DAY 17:
WHO YOU'VE CHOSEN TO BE

"Let us walk properly, as in the day, not in revelry and drunkenness, not in lewdness and lust, not in strife and envy. But put on the Lord Jesus Christ, and make no provision for the flesh, to fulfill its lusts" (Rom. 13:13-14).

Who controls your actions? Have you blamed forces beyond your control? If "It's not my fault!" wasn't your first sentence, that artful dodge was probably your second. You and I don't want to take responsibility for our mistakes. My students are always delighted when I explain that in Spanish, we don't say, "I forgot my home work." The standard construction is more accurately translated, "My homework forgot itself to me."

How that soothes the ego. *Please understand. It's not my fault. There are extenuating circumstances.* My husband has a plaque on his office wall which reads, "If you see a man who's smiling in the midst of misfortune, he's found someone else to blame."

If you don't like who you've become, you can make new choices.

Do you love to play the blame game? I did. Maybe you can relate to some of my reasoning. Of course, I was withdrawn and antisocial. What could you expect of someone who rarely finished the school year in the same school in which she started? Of course, I was absent-minded. Wasn't I frequently scolded? Of course, I burned the stew. How could I know the food was burning if I couldn't smell it? There was *always* an explanation for my shortcomings, and as long as I believed my lies, I remained stuck. To forfeit responsibility is to forfeit control.

The wonderful truth is you are exactly the person *you* have chosen to be. When an ill wind blows into your life, as trouble surely will, you decide what to do about it. If you furl the sails and go below, you will suffer the consequences of your choice to drift on the seas of life without direction. If you reef the sails, don a rain slicker, and man the tiller, you will be wet and tired, but you'll have a chance of ending up where you want to go. If you've turned and run for cover the moment the wind blew cold in your face, you've missed a lot of sunrises.

As for me, losing my friends every few months was hard, but I was the one who decided to avoid the pain of parting by not making new friends. Sure, people found fault with my efforts, but I could have profited from those critiques. (The floor did look smeary the day I mopped the entire house without rinsing the mop.) Sure, I burned the stew. I blamed my culinary disasters on the nasal polyps, which prevented me from smelling, but I could have stayed in the kitchen and stirred the pot instead of retreating to my bedroom to read.

You *have a choice.* What an awesome, horrible, wonderful thought! You can influence your destiny. Neither the mistakes of yesterday nor the ill winds of today can force you into defeat. You *always* have choices. The choices you've made in the past have made you the person you are today, and if you don't like who you've become, you can make new choices. You're free to grow. It's cold up on the deck, and the salt spray stings, but I'm going to put on my yellow slicker, reef the sail, and take the tiller. How about you? You won't regret facing the storm. You'll be proud of yourself.

Day 17: Questions for Reflection

1. How often do you take responsibility for your actions?
2. Who do you blame for your failings?
3. How often do you meet life head-on? Run for cover?
4. What happens when you hide?
5. How pleased are you with who you've become?
6. List the qualities you'd prefer to have.
7. What choices would make you the person you'd like to be?

AFFIRMATION 17:

God will not magically transform me.

Day 18:
Free Will

"Work out your own salvation with fear and trembling; for it is God who works in you both to will and to do for His good pleasure" (Phil. 2:12-13).

Cinderella was my favorite fairy tale, perhaps because I identified with the wretch who did all the work and got nothing in return but a tongue-lashing. Poor thing, always having to obey her wicked stepmother and stepsisters! How the heart stirs to imagine her fairy godmother standing above the ragamuffin, magic wand poised. Poof! A nondescript waif is transformed into a dazzling princess, who goes to the ball without so much as a dancing lesson.

Males aren't immune to the lure of magic. In another popular fairy tale, *Beauty and the Beast*, a handsome prince languishes in the form of a repulsive beast, waiting for the kiss of love to liberate him. He almost dies before he gets the kiss, but then, poof! In a dazzling instant, he is transformed, the ugliness gone forever. Wow! I wanted my life to be a fairy tale. Didn't you? In truth, a bushel basket of kisses has no power to transform your appearance, job description, or destiny. Let's trade in the childish idea of fairy godmothers for a more grown-up concept.

God *does* have the power to transform your dingy life into one of incredible beauty! So, you pray, "Oh Lord, transform me!"

God's working in you demands your cooperation.

Of course, you expect this to be done expeditiously with little or no effort on your part. Poof! Would do very nicely. But the magic never happens. Searching for the reason, you notice, as our scripture for today boldly states, God expects *you* to play a pivotal role in the transformation. There's more. "Do all things without complaining and disputing, that you may become blameless and harmless, children of God without fault in the midst of a crooked and perverse generation, among whom you shine as lights in the world" (Phil. 2:14-15).

In order to shine, you not only have to *work*, but you also have to *obey*! To make matters even less magical, there's fear and trembling involved. You're probably thankful verse thirteen assures God is working in you, but if it's all up to Him, why does He caution against murmuring and disputing? Apparently, God's working in you demands your cooperation. A magical poof won't affect your transformation! You'll have to work through an ongoing process. God *will* transform you when you commit to working with Him. Are you ready?

Day 18: Questions for Reflection

1. In what ways would you like to see your life transformed?
2. How do you envision your transformation taking place?
3. How much of your thinking is magical?
4. In what areas do you most want to shine?
5. What part do you see yourself playing in your transformation?
6. How are you willing to work at transforming yourself?
7. What is preventing you from beginning the work?

AFFIRMATION 18:

I am the person I have chosen to be.

"For the weapons of our warfare are not carnal but mighty in God for pulling down strongholds, casting down arguments and every high thing that exalts itself against the knowledge of God, bringing every thought into captivity to the obedience of Christ" (2 Cor. 10:4-5).

For the first three years I was married, I managed to avoid burning the food. Then the distraction of a six-month-old baby turned the tide. The moment I saw smoke billowing from the frying pan, I heard my mother's voice as clearly as if she were standing beside me. "You burned the supper *again*! You always have your head stuck in a book."

As I turned on the exhaust fan and moved the pan to an empty burner, I marveled at the accuracy of the tape I'd just played. The inflections were so perfect, I was tempted to check behind the fridge to make sure my mother wasn't lurking there. I didn't. *My mother* would never have fit behind the refrigerator. Besides, she was *physically* 2,000 miles away. Mentally, she was closer than my brainwaves. My recordings of her voice played automatically as the situation demanded. I didn't like the direction my mind headed on automatic pilot. How could I regain control?

The apostle Paul speaks of the need to control your thoughts, comparing the effort to a battle requiring weapons only God can provide. "If thoughts of worthlessness are tormenting you, rest assured, those thoughts have not been submitted to Jesus Christ. He established your worth at Calvary. The reason this delirious news hasn't lifted you to cloud nine? Your enemy, variously called the accuser of the brethren and the father of lies, is an expert at criticism. He wants to drive you to depression, but you don't have to listen. You can take your thoughts off autopilot. Tune into the love of God.

You can choose your thoughts.

No one says the battle is easy, but the Bible says you can win. You can choose your thoughts. You are not a dumb animal or an unreasoning automaton. You're a brother or sister of the victorious Lord of heaven and Earth, and God has given you the power of choice.

Day 19: Questions for Reflection

1. Where do your thoughts go on automatic pilot?
2. Who programmed these musings?
3. What does God think about your automatic beliefs?
4. How much territory have you allowed the enemy to occupy?
5. What changes would you like to make in your spiritual weather?
6. How active a role are you willing to play?
7. How do you feel about challenging your unwholesome ideas?

AFFIRMATION 19:

I have the power to change.

Day 20: Positive Thinking

"Fear not, for I am with you; Be not dismayed, for I am your God. I will strengthen you, Yes, I will help you, I will uphold you with My righteous right hand" (Isa. 41:10).

Are you beginning to detect the voice of your inner dictator, shrill and urgent as a smoke detector? "Emergency! Emergency! Act immediately."

The inner dictator batters you into compliance with emotional words, leaving no time for a second opinion. Everything must be decided in the heat of passion, and the principle passion is fear. WHOA! If your foot were wedged in the railroad tracks, and a freight train were bearing down on you, you would be in a real emergency demanding immediate attention.

Most of your life hasn't attained that level of urgency. You have ample time to consult the calm voice of reason, but you may still tend to make emotional decisions. Did you realize you were operating in survival mode? If you want to regain control of your thoughts, you first need to find out who's sitting in the pilot's seat. You may discover you've been hijacked!

The first step to balanced thinking is the realization the shrill voice of alarm is a lie.

To take charge, you'll have to wrest the controls of your life from the hijackers who've commandeered the cockpit. Subduing them won't be easy. Hijackers are always armed, and their principal weapon is fear.

Like a spooky half-light that makes the ordinary seem sinister, fear has you screaming at the sight of a teddy bear. The solution? Turn on the light! Call a time-out. Turn off the speaker blaring the fear message, and take a deep breath. The first thing you'll notice—you're not dead! There's even time for two or three more deep breaths. That shrill voice is a false alarm.

Day 20: Questions for Reflection

1. Which situations cause an alarm to sound in your mind?
2. How mindlessly do you obey your inner voices?
3. What happens when you succumb to fear?
4. What percentage of your decisions are based on fear?
5. What was your last fear-based decision?
6. On what would you prefer to base your decisions?
7. What happens when you try to expose your fears?

AFFIRMATION 20:

I choose to think realistically.

Day 21: The Need to Control

"There are many plans in a man's heart, neverthe-less the LORD's counsel–that will stand" (Prov. 19:21).

How much do you want to control? A few things? Most things? Everything? I thought so. If you're like me, you're much more comfortable when things are under control, *your* control. Okay, I admit it. I'm a control freak. For much of my life, I've done everything in my power to manage everything and everyone around me.

Many people who feel the need to control others assume they have noble motives. They want others to be safe, happy, and healthy, and *they* know exactly how to help. The missing piece is authority. They can only manipulate the lives of others by usurping their authority. God has given each of us the right to govern our own lives, not those of others.

What is the root of my desire to control? A sense that something terrible will happen if I'm not in charge propels me. Knowing my ability to manage things is an illusion doesn't faze my determination. Although my *head* acknowledges I have control over very little, my heart still sinks when I hear of a traffic accident or a murder. *Why didn't I prevent that?* Something blames *me* for the calamity, as though I were in charge of the universe.

Sooner or later, each of us who tries to control the world will meet our Waterloo. My first defeat was associated with my first pregnancy.

No, I didn't crave pickles and ice cream. Not me. I managed what I ate so rigidly, I didn't gain a pound more than the doctor ordered. Yet I approached my ninth month with more than a little trepidation. My fear of death was less troubling than my terror of losing control. Everyone knew women in labor screamed hysterically. *Out* of control!

In 1970, the Lamaze Method was gaining recognition. I received my information on breathing techniques the day I went into labor. When my body shifted into an automatic program I hadn't known existed, I realized I was along for the ride—but not at the wheel. Like a roller coaster, once you get into the car, you relinquish control. When you top the first long hill, you may as well enjoy the wild ride.

On the three-hour drive to the hospital, I read about the Lamaze breathing techniques and attempted them. They helped. I arrived in time for the second stage of my body's programming, push! Demerol and spinal anesthesia blocked the pain. I delivered my son without losing control. Maybe if I *had* screamed, I would have been delivered from the illusion of *being* in control.

God alone is in control, and He does an excellent job of managing all He's created. We learn that lesson sooner or later. Sooner is easier, but I was a slow learner. Twenty-five years later, my marriage ended, and I realized I had zero control. I felt as though the world had turned upside down, and I'd slid off into some cosmic dumpster. I hadn't. God was still on His throne, right where He'd always been. Whew!

Are you ready to give God the wheel, sit in the passenger's seat, and enjoy the scenery?

I am not responsible for floods in China, earthquakes in India, or traffic accidents in my little town of Cottonwood, Arizona. Neither are you. Tragedies don't happen because you failed to pray enough. Abraham, God's friend, interceded long and earnestly for Sodom and Gomorrah, but they burned anyway. God's in charge, and He does what He wants. If you're willing, He'll even take charge of your life. Are you ready to give Him the wheel, to sit in the passenger's seat, and enjoy the scenery?

Each of us is on our own journey, but I'm convinced you and I could shorten our detours by learning from the mistakes of others. That's why I've shared mine with you. I pray you will stay on the straight and narrow way that leads straight to Papa's arms.

Day 21: Questions for Reflection

1. How much control do you *need*?
2. Which areas have you delegated to others?
3. What happens if you stop managing everything?
4. List the things you can direct.
5. List the things you can't influence.
6. Who manages the things you can't?
7. What happens when you try to control others?

AFFIRMATION 21:

I don't need to control everything.

Day 22:
Controlling God

*You ask and do not receive, because you ask amiss,
that you may spend it on your pleasures"
(James 4:3).*

Many Christians struggle to believe that God is good all the time. They don't think God is *bad*. He just seems a bit absent-minded, too preoccupied with the crucial events on Earth to notice their little corner of the planet. They wonder if He's like their parents. Mine withdrew privileges when I failed to meet their desires. How I wished I had known what they wanted. Not knowing made my life unpredictable.

What a relief to discover God wasn't like my parents! He may be different from your parents, too. God communicates His desires. He forgives infractions and never keeps a grudge. He holds you close to His heart. You're important. He won't forget you. When the world beats you up, He bandages your wounds. He *is* trying to give you a blessing. Will you open your hands to receive it?

Don't get me wrong. I'm not saying God doesn't take things away. He does. Like any good parent, he removes distractions that impede His children's growth. The Bible calls this pruning. When I lived in Lodi, California, I was shocked at the extent to which the grape vines were pruned in the fall, but from mere stumps luxurious growth burst forth every spring. God may do some excruciating pruning in your life, but everything He takes away will be something harmful. You may not understand at the time, but everything God does is done in love. He even makes the bad things other people do turn out for your good!

God may do some excruciating pruning.

"And we know that all things work together for good to those who love God, to those who are called according to His purpose .. .. What then shall we say to these things? If God is for us, who can be against us?" (Rom. 8:28,31).

Have you learned you can't control God? He knows exactly what you need, and He delivers your necessities at the best moment. He doesn't need your advice. After all, do you have any clue how to create the world in six days? I didn't think so. You're only pretending if you think you know how to run your life. God, on the other hand, was managing the universe quite well before you were born. You can trust Him. He is good *all* the time.

Day 22: Questions for Reflection

1. How much control did your parents allow you?
2. How do you relate to authority figures?
3. When did God seem to be gracious, capricious, or vindictive?
4. What distasteful experience has God allowed in your life?
5. What was the result of your unsavory experience?
6. What good has come from your misfortunes?
7. How much energy do you expend trying to control God?

AFFIRMATION 22:

DAY 23
CONTROLLING FRIENDS AND FAMILY

"And you, fathers, do not provoke your children to wrath, but bring them up in the training and admonition of the Lord" (Ephesians 6:4).

Life is a conundrum. You and I have amassed a vast library of information we'd love to share with others. Do you feel compelled to tell friends and family what they should eat, how and when they should exercise, and what they should avoid? Withholding this information appears to be gross negligence. How can you stand by and watch your loved ones suffer? If you've had these thoughts, you know how convincing they seem. I'd like to invite you to a conversation I had with my therapist. Come along. I'll sneak you into a session.

"You have little success managing your life because you're expending most of your energy trying to control others."

"Controlling them? I was helping them! Isn't that what friends are for? How could I allow my loved ones to take a wrong turn? With my hand on the wheel, they'll achieve their goals. Or are they my goals? Hmmm. I hadn't thought of that, but without my advice, my daughter might dye her hair green, my son shave his head, or my husband grow a beard."

My counselor stood up and wrote a single word on the white-board: BOUNDARIES.

"I know about boundaries," I assured him. "Before I could build a wall between my house and the neighbor's, I had to locate the boundary pins. After days of digging, I hired a surveyor."

"Why did you want a wall?"

I shrugged. "They keep everyone on their own side, and I'm more comfortable when I know what's mine and what belongs to someone else."

"Exactly," he smiled. "You're not allowing your friends to have fences around their lives. Either they haven't established boundaries, or you've merely climbed over them."

Ahhh! In the end, I realized everyone I knew had made an effort to establish boundaries, but I'd bulldozed them. Those who weren't comfortable with my trespassing had moved away. I'd been wondering where everybody went.

If you can relate to these musings, you may have missed some "No Trespassing" signs yourself. When you start to look for them, you'll be amazed at how many you find. Try announcing to your family that you're resigning from making other people's decisions. I was surprised. My daughter was content with her hair color. My son had no interest in a bald pate, and my husband continued to shave.

Don't get me wrong. Everything didn't go the way I wanted. My son stopped attending church. That was an off-ramp I wouldn't have chosen for him, but it was his decision. That's right—*his*. I no longer feel responsible for other people's decisions, and you don't have to either. Join me in empowering your loved ones to take control of their own lives. You're not accountable for their mistakes, and once they realize *they* are responsible, they'll begin to grow.

You're not accountable for the mistakes of friends and family.

Day 23: Questions for Reflection

---

1. When did you first feel responsible for others?
2. How many people do you feel accountable for today?
3. What are you trying to control about their lives?
4. What successes have you seen?
5. How much energy do you expend to influence others?
6. Which "No Trespassing" signs have you crossed?
7. What boundaries have *you* established?

AFFIRMATION 23:

I refuse to control my friends and family.

Day 24:
Controlling Myself

"But the fruit of the Spirit is love, joy, peace, longsuffering, kindness, goodness, faithfulness, gentleness, self-control. Against such there is no law" (Gal. 5:22-23).

Whose life is easier to manage, yours or someone else's? You may be surprised how much more difficult controlling your own can be. Decisions are more complicated when *you* face the consequences. When you stop trying to control the lives of others, you discover you don't feel as confident about the decisions you make for yourself. You may be frightened when you realize no choice seems foolproof. While you were playing God with others' lives, you felt powerful, not vulnerable. Once you abandon the throne, you feel less competent and more susceptible.

You may decide to ask for advice, only to find the best advice faulty. After consulting a few financial advisors, I invested in several reputable mutual funds. Voila! Within a year, I lost a significant chunk of my investment.

How rarely do we know enough about the issues demanding our decisions! The mind-dizzying number of options available today makes researching each one impossible. Do your best, but don't expect a perfect score. Realizing the mistakes I've made makes me hesitant to offer advice to others.

Major in yourself and let those about you do the same.

Those with small children are voicing protests. Yes, of course, you have to be responsible for the lives of your children. When you hold a newborn in your arms, there is no doubt in your mind that you are 100 percent responsible, but a scant eighteen years later, that child is 100 percent responsible for their own life. What happens in between depends on you.

Some parents keep their children dependent. You've seen the results. Learning to manage your life on the day you leave home ought to qualify as cruel and unusual punishment. A better course is to allow the child to assume a responsibility the moment they demonstrate the ability to handle the job. Thus, they make their mistakes while you're still around to help them clean up the mess.

Perhaps the most important thing for your child is a parent who models control of their own life, gathering information, making decisions, and working through the consequences. Children need to know that making mistakes is part of the learning process. Those who've never made a mistake have never lived. I don't want you or your children to be among them.

How much do you want on your plate? Step back and take a long look at what you want to accomplish in the rest of your life. You can't do everything well, but you can succeed at a few things. You most want to succeed at being yourself: attaining your own dreams and aspirations. I pray you will decide to major in yourself and let those about you do the same. Everyone will benefit. I promise.

Day 24: Questions for Reflection

1. How do you feel about taking charge of your life?
2. How competent are you at making decisions?
3. How do you relate to your mistakes?
4. Are you comfortable allowing your children to mess up?
5. Who have you allowed to control your life?
6. What was the result of giving your power away?
7. What do you choose to be responsible for today?

AFFIRMATION 24:

I can only control one person, myself.

DAY 25: BEING CONTROLLED

"Let nothing be done through selfish ambition or conceit, but in lowliness of mind let each esteem others better than himself" (Phil. 2:3).

Years ago, there was a television advertisement with the unforgettable line, "Mother, I'd really rather do it myself."

Soon, everyone was repeating that universal truth. You and I would rather do it ourselves. From early childhood, we struggled toward independence. At age two, most of us learned to say no, often followed by, "Me do it."

Before you knew how to tie your shoes, you wanted to try. Could you have learned if your parents had insisted on tying those neat little bows for you? Not unless you found a place where you were free to tie some messy bows until you got them right. The same applies to your well-meaning efforts to *help* others: you rob them of the opportunity for growth.

I enjoy playing the piano, even though my musical offerings are sprinkled with mistakes. The congregation for which I play thanks me. Last week, after the service, another pianist plopped a new piece of music in front of me and insisted I play while she sang. I am not great at sight-reading new music, but since we both liked the song, we thought our cooperation would be fun. Wrong! She corrected my playing, calling out the name of each note I missed. I corrected her singing, telling her how and where to breathe. We both gave unsolicited advice, which is *never* a good idea.

Those determined to control us are not really friends.

The person instructing another has set himself up as an expert, which is the opposite of what Paul advises in today's scripture. There is no humility in telling friends or family how they should order their lives. You would do well to ask *their* advice on how to order yours!

How easily do you hold your tongue when you're *sure* you know what another person should do? If you ask permission to offer a suggestion, the other person may say no. Maybe he's having as much fun making mistakes as I do. Rest assured, when he wants your advice, he'll ask for it. In the meantime, you're maintaining a friendship. He feels safe with you. Those around you hate being controlled as much as you do. Those determined to control you are not really your friends.

Day 25: Questions for Reflection

1. What were you *not* allowed to do as a child?
2. How do you feel about being controlled?
3. How do you react when someone tries to dictate to you?
4. Who or what do you try to manage?
5. Why do you try to influence this person or situation?
6. How does your control affect your relationship?
7. When will you focus on managing your own life?

AFFIRMATION 25:

People resent being controlled.

Day 26:
The Power of Choice

"And if it seems evil to you to serve the LORD,
choose for yourselves this day whom you will serve"
(Joshua 24:15).

When I started reading Genesis for the first time, I was shocked. One simple, easily avoidable sin threw God's pristine creation into a hell-bent tailspin. Why didn't the Creator step in? Couldn't God have built a fence around the forbidden tree, removed it from the garden, or made it invisible? He didn't. Couldn't He have knocked the pilfered fruit out of Eve's hand or reiterated His command in case she'd forgotten? Not a whisper. He watched in silence as Eve disobeyed and Adam joined her.

Theologians say God created man with free will, the power of choice. I say that if there was ever an emergency of a magnitude that would justify shelving the concept, it had to be that awful moment when the first sin was about to be committed. God allowed the first humans to eat the forbidden fruit, despite the horrendous price it would cost both them and Him.

Obviously, God places a high premium on this free will of which theologians speak so glibly. If God, who never makes a mistake, isn't willing, even under the direst of circumstances, to infringe on a human's free will, how dare I? Forcing my desires on others robs them of free will, which *includes* the power to choose God.

**Depriving others of their choices puts
you squarely in the enemy's camp.**

One spring morning, as my family was piling into our Nissan for the twenty-minute drive to church, my fifteen-year-old startled us all.

"I'm not going to church today."

I didn't say a word. Many in the congregation criticized me.

"You should have made him come."

Stange, I couldn't imagine Jesus dragging anyone to synagogue. *If he's free to choose to walk away now, he'll be free to choose to come back later.* Besides, what is the benefit of forcing his body to be in church while his heart is somewhere else? God wants the *hearts* of his children: obedience springing from love. "My son, give me your heart, and let your eyes observe My ways" (Prov. 23:26).

You and I cannot comprehend the value God places on free will, but we can choose to respect it. As surely as you regard your free will with awe, you should also regard any desire to manipulate with dread. Depriving others of their choices puts you squarely in the enemy's camp. Satan will then bring you into bondage. He is only too happy to help you control others, even with motives you think noble. True nobility lies in aligning yourself with God. Agree with Him by respecting others, and leave the consequences to Papa.

Day 26: Questions for Reflection

1. How do you feel about free will?
2. When did you force your desires on someone else?
3. What was the result of the coercion?
4. When have others pressed their wishes on you?
5. How did you feel about being coerced?
6. What was the result of your loss of freedom?
7. When should you force your will on another?

AFFIRMATION 26:

Forcing my desires on others is sin.

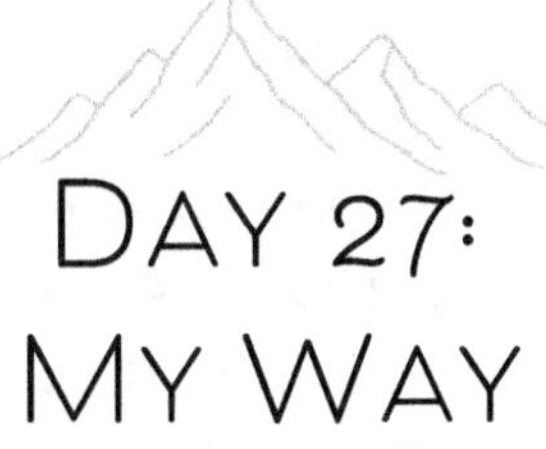

DAY 27:
MY WAY

"For as the heavens are higher than the earth, so are My ways higher than your ways, and My thoughts than your thoughts" (Isa. 55:9).

What happens when you don't get your way? When things spin out of control? When bitter disappointment crowds its unwelcome bulk into your party? This world won't grant your every wish or even most of them. Have you noticed? You plan well, yet the road suddenly takes a turn that wasn't on your map or disappears entirely, washed away in a flood. When your anger runs out of gas, you find yourself far from every point on your itinerary. All is lost. Or is it? Proverbs 16:9 notes, "A man's heart plans his way, but the Lord directs his steps."

Maybe those unplanned diversions aren't catastrophes.

My disaster hit in tenth grade. I had met the love of my life in ninth grade in Deland, Florida, where I had my first opportunity to study a foreign language. Latin? Spanish? French? Hmmm? French! The class was magnifique! Each day, I practiced every new word, and in six weeks, I was chattering in French for half an hour while washing dishes. Then came the move to Simi Valley, California, where the little high school offered *one* foreign language: Spanish. *Bummer!* Devastated, I worked to eliminate the French accent I'd cultivated so painstakingly.

The following summer, we headed north. The high school in Lodi, California, offered two languages: Spanish and German. There would be no returning to my first love. Circumstances dictated that I graduate speaking Spanish, so I took Spanish III and IV simultaneously in my senior year to make up for the year I'd missed. High school hadn't gone as planned.

Like many honor students of the sixties, I entered college as a math major. (We had to catch up with the Russians, who had beaten us into space.) My freshman year, halfway through calculus, I realized a math major would be more work than fun, so I switched to Spanish and earned a Master of Arts degree in the language, which had been my second choice.

If you're delirious with joy in the midst of your trial, you're on the right track.

Today, I'm thankful I was turned away from my beloved French. Spanish is a curriculum staple, and I've been able to find teaching positions in high schools and colleges from Hawaii to Arizona, to say nothing of the years I've spent teaching English to Spanish-speaking students. God's detours are good. They even allowed me to go back to my first love. To major in Spanish, I had to acquire another language, so I minored in French and was privileged to teach it for five years.

The problem with detours is that they don't come neatly packaged with explanations. While you're bumbling through them, you don't know whether or not you'll ever reach the destination *you* had in mind. That's where faith comes in. You either believe God has your best interests at heart or you don't. How can you tell? Check your attitude.

If you're disappointed, you consider your unexpected turn of events a disaster, rather than an opportunity. James counseled: "My brethren, count it all joy when you fall into various trials" (James

1:2), so if you're delirious with joy in the midst of your trial, you're on the right track. Imagine the blessing God is working into you while you wallow in your dilemma.

Day 27: Questions for Reflection

1. Which plan didn't turn out the way you wanted?
2. How have you benefited from this detour?
3. What turned out as planned but wasn't the best?
4. Is there a plan you're fighting to direct today?
5. What's the worst thing that could happen if things don't turn out your way?
6. How have you felt about life's detours?
7. When would you like to flow with God's surprises?

AFFIRMATION 27:

Things don't have to turn out the way I want.

Day 28:
God's Way

"My counsel shall stand, and I will do all my pleasure"
(Isa. 46:10).

"Instead, you ought to say, 'If the Lord wills, we
shall live and do this or that'" (James 4:15).

God is sovereign. He does whatever He wants. The glib assurance, "God's ways are best," slides off the tongue easily in good times, but when your precious plans have capsized, those same words stick in your throat. While you're agonizing over whether to fund a salvage operation or call the undertaker, God's plan is moving ahead at full steam.

God knew before I was born that my family was going to be in Florida when I was in the ninth grade. While we thought we moved from Florida to California the following summer so my pregnant mother could have her baby in a hospital, God had a bigger plan. He not only shifted my focus from French to Spanish, but He also arranged for me to take the SAT in California. My score qualified me for a California State Scholarship, full tuition for four years at the college of my choice! Florida would never have afforded that opportunity, and my family was too poor to fund a college education.

Hindsight is stupendous at figuring out what God had in mind when He pointed your life in a certain direction, but while you're floundering in the wreckage of your shattered dream, you're as blind as a newborn kitten. *Why is this happening? Why can't things go the way I want? Why, God?* Think about it. You wouldn't want to be in control, would you?

Like a newborn kitten, you don't *need* to see. All you need is a wise and loving parent to protect and provide for you. You may not know Him very well yet, but you can be thankful God knows every detail of your life. He's working out the plan He made for you before you were born.

"But now, O LORD, You are our Father; we are the clay, and You our Potter; and all we are the work of Your hand" (Isa. 64: 8).

When I pick up a lump of clay, I begin to roll and pinch it, clumsily attempting to fashion it into a pleasing shape. God does the same with you, except He works with infinite skill. Sometimes the pinching hurts a little. Sometimes it hurts a lot. But always, it serves His glorious purpose—to fashion you into His image.

In the meantime, is there something God is calling you to do? While your loving Father's hand controls every circumstance for your good, you also have a part to play. While I lived in Florida, I went to the library every week and brought home as many books as I could carry. Spending every spare moment reading expanded my vocabulary to the point of excelling on the SAT. What talents and desires has God implanted in you? Use them for His glory.

While you're agonizing over whether to fund a salvage operation or call the undertaker, God's plan is moving ahead at full steam.

Day 28: Questions for Reflection

1. Which circumstances seem out of control?
2. How do you manage your life?
3. How successful have your attempts been?
4. How does God influence your destiny?
5. Who do you wish could influence your direction?
6. How do you feel about being clay in the Potter's hands?
7. Into what shape would you like God to mold you?

AFFIRMATION 28:

God is sovereign.

Day 29:
The Resistance Movement

"Because the carnal mind is enmity against God;
for it is not subject to the law of God,
nor indeed can be" (Rom. 8:7).

Ever since Eve ate the forbidden fruit, humanity has resisted God's rule. Rebellion runs in our veins. Frank Sinatra's hit song, "My Way," expresses the inherent desire of most, a desire that existed long before Old Blue Eyes came on the scene. In an earlier well-known poem, "Invictus," William Ernest Henley vented a fierce determination to control his life. As Henley so eloquently stated, "black as the pit in the fell clutch of circumstance." Hardly a pretty picture.

In my anthology, his prideful poem is followed by a parody entitled "My Captain," Dorothea May's little-known response. Her poem declares Christ the Captain of her soul and describes her path as "bright as the sun." These diametrically opposed poems voice your dilemma. Darkness or light? Your way or God's?

You're tired of your way, but are you tired enough to let go of pride?

Choosing your way is instinctual. You know, you understand, and you see. You're wise, or so you think. You prefer your way to the best way, for no matter how dark, crooked, or tortuous the path, it's yours! You take pride in it. When pride drives you down dark alleys, stop. Are you exalting the troublesome trio: me, myself, and I? Pause. Are you tired? Those twisted paths lead to the horror of darkness. You walk them only because they're the best *you* can find.

The bad news is you haven't the slightest clue how to escape life's dreary maze, but the good news is God knows exactly where the exit is. He's sitting on His throne, high and lifted up, where He can see everything, and if it weren't for pride, you'd long ago have reached up for His hand. He's waiting to lead you into paths of light and glory. The truth is, you're tired of your way, but are you tired enough to let go of pride?

Day 29: Questions for Reflection

1. When did God urge you to do things His way?
2. How do you feel about doing things God's way?
3. When have you done things your way, knowing it opposed God?
4. How easily do you take advice?
5. Which areas of your life suffer from pride?
6. When have you tried to become more humble?
7. How would humility impact your relationships?

AFFIRMATION 29:

My need to control is painful.

Day 30:
A Distant God?

"Be strong and of good courage, do not fear or be afraid of them; for the LORD your God, He is the One who goes with you. He will not leave you nor forsake you" (Deuteronomy 31:6).

I'm worn out. Are you? Controlling others' lives is too much work for anyone. In order to control everything, you first have to be aware of everything. Hyper-vigilance demands gathering all the information possible, but making good decisions requires more than raw information. You also need to understand the nuances of what could be done to improve any situation, as well as the resources available for the task.

I've been told the President of the United States, with all his responsibilities, has to spend hours a day catching up on the data he needs to make wise decisions. Yet, he finds time to take a vacation, play golf, and do other enjoyable things, such as riding a camel in Cairo. Can his job be easier than mine? I have a hard time finding five minutes to sip a lemonade! What am I doing wrong? Or more importantly, what is the President doing right?

Controlling others' lives is too much work for anyone.

In the first place, the President has wisely limited his control by delegating chunks of his responsibility to capable administrators. *He doesn't try to do it all himself.* Secondly, when he has a weighty decision to make, he asks his cabinet, a bevy of competent people who advise him on domestic and foreign affairs. Why didn't I think of that? Probably because I'd have to relinquish a bit of control. That's hard for me. When my husband volunteered to mop the floor, I supervised to make sure he rinsed the mop at proper intervals.

In addition to time and peace of mind, my need to control has robbed me of respect and friendship. Can you imagine how happy my husband was when I pointed out that the mop he was swishing across the tiles was a tad too wet for me? He calls me the inspector general. I don't know who appointed me to that position, but I'm resigning. Who wants endless strain with zero remuneration? As I mentioned, I'm tired, and I'd like to have that lemonade. Who's going to take over? I'll be interviewing applicants as soon as I finish my beverage, and God is first in line. Are you ready to resign?

Day 30: Questions for Reflection

1. Who appointed you inspector general?
2. How pleased are others with your control?
3. How much time do you have for a vacation?
4. Who have you appointed as advisors?
5. How would giving up control improve your relationships?
6. How tired are you? Tired enough to relinquish some control?
7. Under what circumstances would you delegate authority?

AFFIRMATION 30:

Pride resists God.

Day 31:
Relinquishing Pride

"The LORD of hosts has purposed it, To bring to dishonor the pride of all glory, To bring into contempt all the honorable of the earth" (Isa. 23:9).

Pride is a sneaky foe, the master of a thousand faces, one moment urging self-exaltation, the next self-abasement, as in this passage from Hannah Hurnard's classic *Hind's Feet on High Places*. The protagonist, a handicapped maiden named Much-Afraid, has accepted the Shepherd's (Christ's) invitation to the high places. On the way, she has a run-in with her cousin, Pride.

"I thought as much," sneered Pride. "Seeking your heart's desire, eh? And now, Much-Afraid, have a little pride, ask yourself honestly, are you not so ugly and deformed that nobody, even in the Valley, really loves you? That is the brutal truth. Then how much less will you be welcome in the Kingdom of Love, where they say nothing but unblemished beauty and perfection is permitted?"

Poor Much-Afraid! The urge to turn back was almost irresistible, but at that moment, when she stood in the clutch of Pride, feeling as though every word he spoke was the hideous truth, she had an inner vision of the face of the Shepherd, repeating softly, "Behold, thou art fair, my love."

What happened next? Much-Afraid called out to the Shepherd, who clubbed the villain with his staff, and the enemy fled. In another scene, the Shepherd knocked Pride off a cliff into the sea, but the heroine soon spotted her adversary swimming for shore. The Shepherd explained what Much-Afraid already knew: Pride is very hard to kill.

Pride dies a most unwilling death, but once you make the choice, life becomes truly beautiful.

Hurnard does a splendid job of exposing how pride distorts reality. Until pride dies, you will continue to see yourself, your circumstances, and other people in the glass of a carnival mirror, which makes little things seem huge and big things tiny. Pride's agenda is simple: to keep you satisfied with yourself, so you won't ask for the help you need.

The first step of the highly successful Twelve-Step Program is an admission of powerlessness. Step one signals the death of pride. Alcoholics call the realization they can't make it on their own "hitting bottom." Some people have to hit rock bottom before they realize they've fallen all the way to the gutter.

I had to lose the vision in one eye before I realized I was powerless. Even then, I found listening to others difficult. Obeying God can be even harder. Pride dies a most unwilling death. Only after the carnival mirror is smashed can life become truly beautiful. Won't you join me in this moment of painful reality?

Day 31: Questions for Reflection

1. Who suggested your reality may be distorted?
2. How do you feel when corrected?
3. In which areas do you feel important? Unimportant?
4. What has pride cost you?
5. When did you think pride had left you?
6. At what time did you suffer the least from pride?
7. In what area is pride the worst problem?

AFFIRMATION 31:

Pride must die before God can rule.

Day 32:
Humility's Reward

"Humble yourselves in the sight of the Lord, and He
will lift you up" (James 4:10).

You and I love humility. It's so comfortable. When you're humble, you're relieved of the need to solve everyone else's problems. You don't feel compelled to share your opinion or give advice. You don't even have to solve all your own problems.

You have choices, lots of them. You can commit your problems to God by writing them on slips of paper, dating them, and dropping them into a "God box," any container big enough to hold all your troubles. (I keep a separate dated list of what I've thrown into the container so I can remind myself not to worry about those issues.) Then you wait patiently for God's solution to unfold in His time. Alternatively, you may choose to ask advice from those around you who have dealt with a similar issue, or if no one is available, search the Internet for ways others have solved related problems. Lastly, you may choose to leave your difficulty unresolved, humbly admitting you *don't* know what to do. *Who said you should be able to solve every issue?*

Humility proves elusive.
You may have to re-choose it often.

When I'm in humble mode, I feel light and whole, at one with God. Humility puts me in touch with my Creator. I am the creature of His hand, the sheep of His pasture, dependent on Him to supply all I need. Dependency has gotten a bad rap lately, but the dependency to which I'm referring is not harmful. Dependency is reality. When I admit I need help, I'm acknowledging my true identity.

Unfortunately, humility proves elusive. You may have to re-choose it, sometimes quite often. You may go to bed humbly submitted to God, at peace with your problems, and confidently awaiting God's solutions, only to awaken in a panic, mind whirling with disastrous possibilities. During the night, pride has crept in, insisting *you should know what to do and do it immediately.* The solution? Choose humility *again.*

Remind yourself you're neither Superman nor Wonder Woman, and you don't have all power. You're not even all-wise. God is. And He's taken your problems into His great big hands. Whew! Although the butterflies in your stomach may not escape the moment you realize God has sent His angels to watch over you, most of them quickly settle down.

When you're not focused on your difficulties, they tend to fade. You're looking upward, which is always a great place to look. Whether the sky is clear and blue or gray with storm clouds, you can be certain that beyond the reach of your earthbound eyes lies glory indescribable. God is there, holding your problems in His capable hands.

Day 32: Questions for Reflection

1. How have you gotten into a humble mode?
2. How pleasant did you find humility?
3. When was your last truly carefree moment?
4. How often do you feel like Superman?
5. What do you feel compelled to control?
6. When did you leave your problems in God's hands?
7. When would you like to give humility a try?

AFFIRMATION 32:

When pride is dead, the war is over.

Day 33: God's Requirement

"He has shown you, O man, what is good; And what
does the LORD require of you but to do justly, to
love mercy, and to walk humbly with your God"
(Micah 6:8).

What does vanquishing pride have to do with escaping perfectionism? Everything! Pride is the driving force behind the quest for applause. When I thought I was going after what was best for my family, I was really thinking about something entirely different. *What would the neighbors think? What would my family say? How would my friends react?* Even total strangers made the endless list of people I felt I needed to impress.

A proud person feels compelled to make a good showing at *all* times. In the process, they compromise their authenticity, peace of mind, and energy. Enough! Let's ask a few questions. Who are these *others* you feel so compelled to please? Why do you need to impress them? Do you want your life to be ruled by people you may not even know? If your answer is no, you may be ready for an adventure into inner space.

The perfectionist experiences a constant tension between who she really is and the image she feels compelled to project. This uncomfortable split is deemed necessary because she is convinced the real (imperfect) self is unacceptable and therefore unlovable. And she, like every human being, needs love! Teenagers who brave the pain of piercing tender lips and tongues give us a glimpse of how much discomfort a human will endure to gain the acceptance of their peers.

Though you may think the teen is paying too high a price for approval, pierced tongues heal in four hours once the pin is removed, or so a recently-pierced lass informed me. The perfectionist, on the other hand, pays an unending price. Her entire life is skewed. A person who can't be true to herself can't be true to the world around her or the God who made her.

The bad news is you will never achieve perfection. Falling short is the best *you* can do. You're human. The good news is that God isn't human. He's the perfect One! He always has been, and He always will be. But that's not all. If you choose to surrender your life to Him, He will transform you into His image, relentlessly working His spotless perfection into your life.

Admit you're not perfect. Stop pretending you can get along without God. Confess the failure you've made of your life, and accept His help. Once you do, He'll transform you, slowly but surely, into His glorious image. Now that's perfection.

Perfectionists experience a tension between who they are and the image they project.

Day 33: Questions for Reflection

1. Are you ready to surrender your pride?

    If you answered yes to that question, you may want to pray this humble prayer:

    Lord, I've made a mess of my life. Forgive me. I see now I'll never be perfect. I need Your help every day. I give up trying to be something I'm not. Please take my life and make me authentic, true to myself and true to others, but most of all, true to You.

2. If you answered no to the first question, what advantage do you see in holding onto pride?

AFFIRMATION 33:

I put pride to death every day.

DAY 34:
ABSOLUTE SURRENDER

"But Jesus said to him, 'No one, having put his
hand to the plow, and looking back, is fit
for the kingdom of God'" (Luke 9:62).

Most of us have some notion that throwing our lot in with God involves surrender. How complete each surrender must be is understood differently by various churches, and even by assorted Christians sitting in the same church. As a teenager, I observed some Christians who seemed more "all in" than others. They disrupted their lives to go to the mission field. Others couldn't commit to weekly church attendance. I wondered if people progressed to deeper levels of commitment or just stayed where they were.

The night before a serious eye surgery, these questions came to a head. I sat on my bed and read Andrew Murray's priceless little volume, *Absolute Surrender*, written in 1895 and published in the US by Bethany House. If I could never read again, I wanted his words imprinted on my mind. The analogy of the pencil was unforgettable. I couldn't locate it again, so I've reconstructed my version.

Whether I jot down a grocery list, a love letter, or an apology, the pencil in my hand is completely surrendered to my will. I am free to write whatever I please. I'm not one to gnaw on the wood or nibble the eraser, but if I were, my pencil would not protest. Writing to-do lists, or senseless scribbles, is all the same because my writing implement has no agenda of its own, no union card with a job description, no report to the authorities of abuse. I'm free to poke that submitted cylinder into the soil of a potted plant to prop up a droopy stem. That analogy challenges me.

I've made countless "absolute" surrenders, only to discover there was something I'd reserved for myself. *I'm willing to be a pencil in your hand, Lord, but don't put me in someone else's hand. I want to write sweet notes of encouragement, but don't ask me to inventory fan belts, and please, oh please, don't throw me into a greasy toolbox!*

The words of Frances Ridley Havergal's hymn "Live Out Thy Life Within Me" eloquently express the conditions of absolute surrender. He describes the body as a slave to Christ with the words: "Ready to have Thee use me or not be used at all."

Searching for peace?
Try absolute surrender.
There is no substitute.

Those lyrics were written in 1864. Are you living them today?

The surrendered life is peaceful, devoid of restlessness, strain, or regret. I know. I've tried it. The perfect peace you've been searching for is available today. Once you yield unconditionally, God takes responsibility for your life. You're in His hands, like clay on a potter's wheel. Don't worry about what He'll make of you. His plans are always magnificent. If you, my friend, have been searching for peace, try absolute surrender. There is no substitute.

Day 34: Questions for Reflection

1. How much peace do you experience?
2. How peaceful would you like to be?
3. What robs you of peace?
4. Which areas of your life have you surrendered?
5. What was the result of your capitulation?
6. When you don't yield, what happens?
7. What frightens you about surrender?

AFFIRMATION 34:

My surrender must be absolute.

Day 35: The Problem of Withholding

"I beseech you therefore, brethren, by the
mercies of God, that you present your bodies
a living sacrifice, holy, acceptable to God,
which is your reasonable service" (Rom. 12:1).

If you remember the Hebrew sacrificial system, you understand that every sacrifice died. Some were burned up, others eaten, but all died. Nothing was withheld. If you attend church, you've probably heard some version of the oft-repeated story that illustrates the concept of withholding. A Christian hears a knock on the door. Jesus asks to come in. The man is delighted to receive the Lord.

Jesus then asks for access to the desk. Again, the person readily agrees. After all, this is God. Finally, Christ asks for the key to a certain little drawer. The Christian hesitates. *Wait a minute. That's a hard thing. Those are special treasures. Why do You have to have everything? Can't You be content with 97 percent?*

Instinctively, you sympathize. At one time or another, you've had that drawer. *I'm yours, Lord, at least most of me is. Just don't ask me to surrender this one tiny thing. This is embarrassing. I know I really shouldn't be hanging onto that, but I'm not ready to give it up.*

God is so picky—the Bible calls it jealous. He demands everything.

If you're not remembering the "desk" version of this story, you may have heard the "house" version, in which the Christian is willing to surrender every room except one small closet. Don't waste time calculating whether you could fit more into a closet than a drawer. The point is not how *much* is withheld but whether *anything* is withheld.

God is so picky. The Bible calls it jealous. He demands everything. Absolute surrender pleases Him because only absolute surrender produces the results He desires. Then the answers are all yes. "Yes, Lord, come in. Yes, here are the keys. Yes, everything belongs to You. Yes, You may do whatever You want with me and all I possess."

Saying yes to God can be excruciating until you've grasped the simple truth that surrendering to Him makes you richer, not poorer. Much richer! Jesus told two stories that illustrate this concept. In one, a merchant sells everything to buy a pearl of great price. In the other, a man who finds a treasure in a field, buries it again, quickly sells everything, and buys the field.

Did these men agonize over their decisions? No! They were anxious to complete the transactions because the breathtaking treasures they were acquiring were much more valuable than the things they had sold. Did you notice? In both stories, they had to sell *everything they owned*. God wants absolute surrender, and until you make that decision, He won't be satisfied, and neither will you.

Do you have a "secret" drawer? That secret will cause untold misery. Ask God to reveal the contents of your hidden stash. You may laugh at their triviality or cry at their preciousness, but your reaction will be inconsequential. You don't want emotions to run your life. Like the biblical merchant, sell everything and buy the greatest treasure. Not only is the pearl of great price a wonderful bargain today, it's guaranteed to appreciate tremendously over the next few years.

Day 35: Questions for Reflection

1. How do you feel about God wanting 100 percent?
2. When have you considered absolute surrender?
3. How did you feel about giving up everything?
4. What's in your secret drawer?
5. How easily could you surrender everything?
6. What do you value most highly?
7. Have you had a glimpse of the pearl of great price?

AFFIRMATION 35:

I ask God to reveal anything I'm holding back.

DAY 36: OUR SUPERHERO

"He shall call upon Me, and I will answer him; I will be with him in trouble; I will deliver him and honor him" (Ps. 91:15).

Maybe you've seen the 1985 film *Runaway Train*. The opening scene showed the demise of the engineer, who tumbled off the train. At first, no one realized the locomotive was out of control, careening down the mountain at an ever-increasing speed. By the time a few people understood the gravity of the situation, a fiery crash seemed inevitable. Those in the know struggled with the decision of whether to derail the train to spare the town at the bottom of the hill.

To save the train, the hero had to drop from the sky onto the roof and fight off the bad guys. Can you identify with his dilemma? Does your life feel as though it's lacking direction? Do you have the premonition that the person who should be at the wheel is somehow missing? Have you tried everything to slow your downward momentum with no success?

Maybe you do see one desperate solution, but you don't feel like a hero. Perhaps you even deal with a hearty streak of cowardice and wouldn't consider dropping from a helicopter onto the top of a speeding train. Is the situation hopeless?

No. The situation is not hopeless, though *you* may have tried every solution in your toolbox. If you're good at derailing your life, getting sidetracked into addiction, or distracted by trivial pursuits with no return for eternity, you're in good company. Getting distracted is easy. Satan makes sure of that. Getting focused may appear impossible. The devil is very good at what he does!

The Lord is my Shepherd, and I'm His sheep.

Fortunately, nothing is impossible with God. You have a Champion who's proven Himself brave enough, strong enough, and smart enough to regain control of your life. Although He's the best Engineer in the world, He works for nothing. The catch? It's that 100 percent thing again. Until you make an absolute surrender, you're still careening downhill, headed for the abyss.

I praise God that He was willing to stop my downward slide, turn me around, and head me toward heaven. My life has been amazing since that moment. I'm not perfect, but I'm no longer plunging downhill. The Lord is my shepherd, and I'm His sheep, depending on Him for everything. And you, my friend? Which way are you heading?

Day 36: Questions for Reflection

1. How much of your life have you surrendered?
2. Who do you know whose life seems out of control?
3. In which areas are you careening toward the abyss?
4. Which areas seem well controlled?
5. Who's been managing your life?
6. What qualifications have you set for a manager?
7. How difficult do you find God's directions?

AFFIRMATION 36:

I thank God for being willing to direct my life.

DAY 37: HIDING

"For there is nothing covered that will not be revealed, nor hidden that will not be known. Therefore, whatever you have spoken in the dark will be heard in the light, and what you have spoken in the ear in inner rooms will be heard on the housetops" (Luke 12:2-3).

In John Powell's popular little book, *Why Am I Afraid to Tell You Who I Am?*, the Jesuit priest answers the title question with the obvious: I'm afraid that if you know who I *really* am, you won't love me. Have you felt that way, at least in critical situations? Most hesitate to reveal too much, lest the other decide they don't want to be their friend, companion, or lover. They wear a carefully constructed persona. Some even consider themselves repulsive enough to change the ways they look, speak, and act.

These concerns are exaggerated. Since the person to whom you're confessing your shortcomings has his own defects, admitting your foibles often brings a reciprocal confession and the healing realization that you are not alone. Others also struggle with temptation and suffer from checkered pasts, so what you suspect might separate you may be the key to bringing you closer.

Regret is the reason you want to hide.

That reasoning doesn't work with Almighty God. The sinless One is repulsed by evil. Worse yet, trying to keep a secret from Him is ludicrous. God knew every sin you'd commit before you were born. Yet, He has chosen to forgive and forget them. Then He invites you to forget them, too. In 2 Corinthians 7:10, the apostle Paul states that sorrow according to the will of God produces repentance *without* regret.

Regret is why you want to hide, so how do you stop regretting? You've made horrendous mistakes that disgraced God and hurt others. To stop berating yourself, you must believe all things *do* work together for good to those who love God. Then, you must trust that He is able to bring great good out of your personal evil. Finally, you must thank Him for the blessings He's growing out of the ashes of your sins. Appreciation is excellent fertilizer.

The God who appointed Moses's brother Aaron Israel's first high priest, soon after he'd led the people in a pagan worship service, is ready and willing to forgive your sins. Wouldn't you be a fool to hold on to a past that drives you into hiding? Forget your yesterdays, and step into today.

Day 37: Questions for Reflection

1. How do you feel about your past?
2. What would you rather hide, even from God?
3. What confidence has a friend betrayed?
4. How does God forget the sins we confess?
5. What sins have you forgotten?
6. What benefits have regrets brought?
7. When will you be ready to let the past go?

AFFIRMATION 37:

God knows all about me, but never gives up.

DAY 38: WHO'S IN CHARGE?

"A man's heart plans his way, but the
LORD directs his steps" (Prov. 16:9).

Most Christians would express delight at having God in control of our lives, but a little reflection reveals a few things we would prefer to control ourselves—quite a few. This desire persists even though we realize we will suffer loss as a result of our incompetence. Our best efforts fall short of the managerial skills of the Controller of the universe.

When I applied for a teaching position at the Community College of Southern Nevada, I felt I had a fair chance of being selected. I had been working there as an adjunct professor for over a year with excellent evaluations. What I didn't realize was that the position had been advertised all over the world, and more than two hundred people, anxious to move to Las Vegas, had applied.

I made the first cut and was one of five applicants interviewed by the college president. Things were looking up! I made the final cut, one of four who presented a lesson to the faculty. The college hired the chairman of the University of Nevada's Spanish Department, a charismatic native speaker who was completing her PhD. Had I known this superstar had applied, I might not have wasted my time.

Objectively, she was the best choice. I could do little but applaud the decision. She had had the position in her pocket before it was advertised, but in the end, whose decision was it? God knew my best interest was *not* to remain in Las Vegas, where I would have retired fifteen years later. Instead, He led me to Arizona the following year.

Whose hand should guide your life?

Whose hand should guide your life? Applicants for the position would be few: God, Satan, and yourself. (Family and friends are usually too wise to want such a thankless task.) You'd disqualify Satan right off. You don't want the devil in control of your life, not for a second. You might like to fool around in his playground, but you don't want to get locked in with him when the curtain falls on Earth's drama.

That leaves two possibilities: God, Creator and Sustainer of the universe, and you, a limited human being. The choice is more obvious than who should have been hired for the teaching position at the community college. Now we come to you. Have you made the logical choice? God knows all about you and still loves you. He always has your best interest at heart, and He's fully capable of managing your affairs. What more could you ask?

Day 38: Questions for Reflection

1. Name those who run your life today.
2. How satisfied are you with their management?
3. What have you asked God to control?
4. Which areas of life do you prefer to manage?
5. What do you fear God would do in those areas?
6. When has your Father let you down?
7. What prevents your surrender to God?

AFFIRMATION 38:

I want God to direct my life.

Day 39:
Safe at Last!

"The name of the LORD is a strong tower; the righteous run to it and are safe" (Prov. 18:10).

Have you had the misfortune of riding with someone whose driving left you terrified? Maybe you wore a hole in the floorboards trying to apply the nonexistent passenger-side brakes. Few have the ability to emerge from a hair-raising drive with poise. We long for the illusion of safety we feel when we're at the wheel. Our flawed logic runs something like this: *I need to be in control so I can be safe.* If that sounds reasonable, you may be suffering from some of the same delusions the rest of us harbor.

In reality, being in control brings safety *only* when the controller:

1. Has the ability to foresee all difficulties.
2. Possesses the power to avert all problems.
3. Dedicates his entire time and energy to avoiding trouble.

In other words, being safe requires both omniscience and omnipotence. Obviously, God is the only Being capable of protecting anyone. I am fascinated that He has chosen to endure some horrendous trials. Few situations would activate *my* desire to seize control more than watching my precious son cruelly murdered. Yet Almighty God, easily able to avert the crucifixion, chose not to do so. He stood by, heart torn by agony. That boggles my mind.

The crucifixion challenges you to look beyond the desire to save your own skin. Jesus judged the reward of His suffering to be worth the price He paid. Your mind may stagger when you realize the reward for which He endured such torture was you. Yes, you! Since He paid such an excessive price to ransom you, have no fear that He will abandon you to the whims of cruel fate. He has unlimited resources to protect you. As the psalmist observed: "The angel of the LORD encamps all around those who fear Him, And delivers them" (Ps. 34:7).

If you're on God's team,
He has to be the Coach.

Being on God's team has some unbelievable perks, but if you're on *His* team, *He* has to be the Coach. Since you are neither omniscient nor omnipotent and require many hours of sleep as well as other downtime, you are not capable of protecting yourself. Besides, your store of willpower is easily exhausted, leaving you vulnerable.

As much as I wanted to finish this page before I turned in for the night, I've dozed off at the keyboard several times, producing lines full of the same letter. I really *can't* control myself, and neither can you. Will you trust God to control the things you can't? Move over and let Him drive.

Day 39: Questions for Reflection

1. Which issues do you attempt to manage?
2. How much stress do they add to your life?
3. What would happen if you released control?
4. How much influence do you really exercise?
5. How much responsibility do you want?
6. When do you feel most peaceful?
7. When do you feel most stressed?

AFFIRMATION 39:

I can learn to feel safe when God's in control.

Day 40:
God's Plan

"For I know the thoughts that I think toward you, says the LORD, thoughts of peace and not of evil, to give you a future and a hope" (Jer. 29:11).

Trusting God is easy when we're talking generalities. Sure, you trust Him. You trust Him to bring the sun up in the morning and make spring follow winter. You've never lost sleep worrying that the moon might crash into the Earth. God manages the trajectories of heavenly bodies with no assistance on your part. He was on the job eons before you were born and hasn't taken so much as a coffee break, but He's never made an error. He's perfect! Moses understood God's ways.

"He is the Rock, His work is perfect; For all His ways are justice, A God of truth and without injustice; Righteous and upright is He" (Deuteronomy 32:4).

Although I wouldn't presume to advise God on how to manage the universe, I feel differently when my life is involved. There are times when I dare to express my suggestions. Sometimes, I hate to admit, I even grumble.

The first time you read the account of God accosting Moses at the burning bush, you may snicker. What a jerk! Moses has the nerve to argue with the Almighty! He suggests that God has picked the wrong man and all but turns down the most significant assignment of the age. What's the matter with this hero-to-be? Ah! He doesn't know the end of the story.

All Moses knows is that he has a neat little plan worked out for his life, and his plan doesn't include traipsing back to Egypt, where there's a price on his head. He's old, comfortable, and handicapped with a nasty fear of public speaking. He trusts God in a general way, sure! But as far as leaving his whole life behind—his reaction is a polite, "Send somebody else."

The problem with God is that He's not controllable. He stands above all, demanding to be Lord of all. You can't submit to *His* lordship and pick your assignment. Moses eventually submitted, but not until he'd wheedled himself into a helper. His brother Aaron made the golden calf at Mount Sinai and led Israel in a pagan worship service. That debacle ended with Moses smashing the tablets on which God had written the Ten Commandments. I wonder how many times Moses wished he'd let God have His way from the beginning.

Don't make Moses's mistake of telling God what's best. You want to entrust the details of your life and the lives of those you love to God. If He asks you to pack up at a moment's notice and move, is that okay? After moving out of the house where I'd pressed my baby's footprints into wet cement, I've discovered that no subsequent place really feels like home. At first, I felt sad. Then I realized—no place on Earth *is* home.

My dwelling is on the other side. Where I camp until I get there or what my tent looks like doesn't matter. Not really. What about you? Are you keeping your eye out for burning bushes? When you give God the reins of your life, you're in for a wild ride, but you'll learn a lot. Don't miss the adventure.

When you give God the reins of your life, you're in for a wild ride.

Day 40: Questions for Reflection

1. Who do you consult when you have a decision to make?
2. What might God say if you asked Him?
3. What suggestions do you make to God?
4. Have you declined an invitation to adventure?
5. If so, what do you think you missed?
6. What tempts you to sit on the sidelines?
7. How far are you willing to go with God?

AFFIRMATION 40:

Trusting God is more difficult than I realized.

Day 41: Relinquishing Control

"Let this mind be in you which was also in Christ Jesus, who being in the form of God, did not consider it robbery to be equal with God, but made Himself of no reputation, taking the form of a bondservant, and coming in the likeness of men" (Phil. 2:5-6).

Okay, let's admit it: we may never have actually handed the reins of our lives over to God for more than a split second. Oh, we've tried lots of times. But making the decision is one thing. Following through is another. Have you experienced courage melting into cowardice? I did.

I'd watched my three children take the plunge off the high dive into the Kaneohe District Park pool. They loved it. The high dive was a treat. So, one afternoon, I shinnied up the ladder. Big mistake! Climbing the stairs announced to the whole world–or at least everyone in the pool–that *I* was planning to jump. I walked to the edge of the turquoise diving board and hung my toes over the abyss. My heart sank. The water was way down there.

As I contemplated slinking back down the ladder, my older son began to cheer, "Come on, Mom, you can do it. Go for it, Mom!"

Ah, for the valor of a six-year-old! I jumped. What else could I do? I'm sure my heart stopped the microsecond I stepped off the platform. The water hit me hard, stinging my face and driving burning chlorine up my nose. I didn't care. The ordeal was over, and I'd learned my lesson. Never climb the ladder again!

My experience differed significantly from that of my second son. I listened in awe later that afternoon as Ken described jumping off the platform, tucking his head, twisting his body, aligning his feet, and entering the water at a precise angle. What did he do? Fall in slow motion? Where did he find the time to give his body all those commands and carry them out in the seconds before he dipped gracefully into the water? My four-year-old was not afraid.

When terror's icy fingers grip you, you can no longer trust your senses. Surging adrenaline flushes the last traces of objectivity, and you are sucked into an emotional maelstrom of your own creation. Your heart races. You experience a sinking feeling. Have you been there?

I experience this sinking feeling each time I contemplate abandoning myself to God. My lips declare, "Here I am, Lord. Take me. I trust You. Do whatever You want."

About that time, a snide little voice wheedles, "Think before you make such a rash decision! Surrendering to God is hazardous. Who knows what He'll ask? What if he wants a martyr?"

Make the mistake of listening to that voice, and your courage ebbs. You may even recant, consoling yourself that yes, of course, you want to submit to God—eventually.

What empowers you to follow wherever God leads? When you become so hungry for your Father's embrace that you don't count the cost, fear evaporates. Like the prodigal, you decide to head home, come hell or high water. Even if your fears are serious, God's way is the only way through them. With His Father's help, Jesus navigated hell, and Israel marched through high water. What do you fear?

**Even if your fears are serious,
God's way is the only way through them.**

Day 41: Questions for Reflection

1. Which fears impede your surrender?
2. When will you discuss your trepidations with God?
3. Are your feelings logical or emotional?
4. What could you do if you were fearless?
5. How have you confronted your anxieties?
6. What was the result of your tactic?
7. What are you willing to pay for a fearless life?

AFFIRMATION 41:

I fear God's control because I haven't tried it.

Day 42:
Learning to Trust

"But as for me, I trust in You, O LORD; I say, 'You are my God.' My times are in Your hand; Deliver me from the hand of my enemies, And from those who persecute me" (Ps. 31:14-15).

Sensitive individuals try to control every aspect of their environments, their minds continually scanning for threats and devising escape plans. While others enjoy a celebration, they stand guard like secret service agents at a presidential dinner. They may eat the caviar or drink the champagne, yet scarcely taste them, while an endless stream of data overwhelms their senses.

Seated in a booth at a Las Vegas buffet, I listened with half an ear to my husband's cheery review of the delights of salmon steaks and cherry cheesecake. Why did he have to mention the recent fire in a casino kitchen? This casino kitchen! Once I grasped that the kitchen fire had quickly spread to the dining room, resulting in multiple deaths, I couldn't relax until I'd devised an escape route. Are you as cautious as I am?

Some people assume they'll win the door prize and often do. Luck follows them like a butler, tending to their every need. They feel blessed. Others are equally certain they *won't* win anything and never do. Disaster follows them, spoiling their plans and ruining their relationships. They feel *cursed*. These unfortunates consider themselves the most likely to be struck by lightning. They are disaster magnets.

Give up guard duty. Standing watch is senseless if the unexpected happens anyway.

The blessed are willing to take chances, assuming that if anything bad happens, it will happen to someone else. The cursed know they're the "someone else" to whom bad things happen. Fearful and exhausted, they have become Eeyore, the stuffed donkey from Milne's Winnie-the-Pooh books.

How does a person become gloomy? Alcoholic parents? Childhood abuse? Trauma? Rejection? Betrayal? A horrendous loss? A loss of something irreplaceable or someone precious is always involved: a parent, a best friend, one's innocence, or one's childhood.

No matter what may have contributed to your gloomy outlook, you alone are responsible. You decided to insulate yourself against the pain of dashed hopes by expecting the worst, and the worst happens more often when you anticipate it. Beleaguered Job stated: "For the thing I greatly feared has come upon me, and what I dreaded has happened to me" (Job 3:25).

Like Job, you attract things you fear, yet God promises: "All things work together for good to those who love God" (Rom. 8:28).

Could that mean God allows you to attract things you fear so you can overcome them? Scripture promises that perfect love casts out fear. I've learned one thing from my ceaseless vigilance: I *can't* protect myself. Accidents are over in a split second. Only God, who operates with split-second timing, can prevent them.

I suggest you give up. If the unexpected is going to happen anyway, standing watch is senseless. You're due for a change; the change from relying on yourself to relying on God. Rest assured that He never sleeps. He always has His eye on you.

Day 42: Questions for Reflection

1. What frightens you about God?
2. Which part of your life do you want God to protect?
3. How successful have you been in defending yourself?
4. How well have you succeeded in shielding others?
5. How much do you rely on God to take care of you?
6. Which area of your life demands the most energy?
7. Why do you feel your life is blessed? Or cursed?

AFFIRMATION 42:

I trust God to take charge of my life.

Day 43: Safe in God's Hands

"God is our refuge and strength,
A very present help in trouble" (Ps. 46:1).

Why try to control things when moments of success are swallowed by seasons of failure? The logical brain would give up, but vigilance is a deeply ingrained gut reaction. Here's a simple tool I read somewhere to uncover the root of the problem: write down the perplexing behavior, followed by the word "because." Finish the sentence. Then add "because" to the next sentence and keep going until the driving motive behind the seemingly irrational behavior emerges. The last sentence will not contain the word "because."

My own process spilled onto the paper something like this:

I try to control everything <u>because</u> I *need* order.

I need order <u>because</u> I feel uncomfortable in messy surroundings.

I feel uncomfortable in messy surroundings <u>because</u> disorder means *I've* lost control.

I need to be in control <u>because</u> when *I'm* not managing things, someone else is.

I feel uncomfortable when someone else is managing things <u>because</u> that person may not like me.

If the person in control doesn't like me, he or she may harm or even kill me.

Eureka! My need for control was rooted in an irrational fear of being hurt or killed if I didn't please the person over me. That fear was rooted in a childhood experience I hadn't even remembered until God showed me I had almost choked to death when I was five. Even then, I didn't realize my early trauma was still influencing me. Once I saw the connection, I was able to break free.

Your process may come to a different conclusion, but once the root of your uneasiness has been uncovered, you can dig it out. You need to dig with the patience, persistence, and determination of a prisoner digging an escape tunnel because that's exactly what you're doing.

You can reprogram yourself for reality by embracing truth and logic. In my case, I asked myself whether I would really die if I indulged in a carefree moment. My logical mind said no. Although my first happy-go-lucky moments lasted only seconds, those seconds gave me a glimpse of a different realm. With a little persistence, I expanded those five seconds to five minutes and then five hours. The process was liberating.

Jesus explained there were two kinds of people in a house: slaves and sons. Hmmm. If you have lived like a slave, driven by forces beyond your understanding, it's time to move into your true position as a son. You are a child of the King.

Let hope keep you digging toward the light, where life is free and full. Once you've escaped, you may want to run through puddles in the rain. To get up before dawn to look at the stars. To giggle for no reason at all. You can learn to trust others and relinquish control to God. And no, you won't die. You'll begin to live. Are you ready to plan your escape?

Let hope keep you digging toward the light, where life is free and full.

Day 43: Questions for Reflection

1. When did you first feel a need to manage everything?
2. How much control do you need to feel comfortable?
3. How productive and enjoyable is your life?
4. How often do you feel a need to remain vigilant?
5. Does logic agree that you need to be in charge?
6. When was your last carefree moment?
7. What would happen if you were less serious?

AFFIRMATION 43:

**God can do a better job
of protecting me than I can.**

Day 44:
Giving Up Control

"Trust in the LORD with all your heart, And lean
not on your own understanding; In all your ways
acknowledge Him, And He shall direct your paths"
(Prov. 3:5-6).

Somebody has to be in control, or the world spins into chaos. Have you ever wanted someone to be you? There have been times when I was charged with a task I couldn't accomplish. One sunny Sunday afternoon in Waimanalo, Hawaii, a half-dozen parishioners were attempting to raise the roof of a sizable building we were constructing behind the sanctuary. The roof was a complex hip-and-valley design with several different sizes of trusses.

The first step was to hoist the main trusses, which were longer than the width of the building, and jockey them into position, hanging them upside down on the cement-block walls. Several extra hands had turned up for this task, which resembled getting an oversized piece of furniture down a narrow hall and through a tiny doorway. The newcomers all looked to me, one of the four regulars on the job, for direction.

Blazing your own trail is much harder than following a good leader.

Spatial relations have always been a mystery to me. I hated those questions on the elementary school IQ tests that showed pictures of hands. *Is this a right hand or a left hand?* How could anyone know? Eventually, I figured out to look at *my* hands to see which one matched the picture, but first I had to figure out which was my right hand. Obviously, I was not the person to give directions to these men.

We got the first truss up with no problem. But how to maneuver the second one into position with the first one blocking the way? I had those men jockeying that truss in every direction except the one that would work. Mercifully, a fellow with excellent spatial relations shooed me off the job and took my place. The roof was raised that afternoon.

I was greatly relieved to be fired. In retrospect, I wonder why I even tried. People were looking to me, expecting me to be able to do the task. Maybe you, like me, find yourself in the driver's seat when you know the person sitting next to you could do a better job. That's especially true when the person sitting next to you is our Lord Jesus Christ.

Have you wasted time, energy, and resources insisting on being in charge? If so, you're probably tired. Blazing your own trail is much harder than following a good leader. Are you ready to let someone else take over?

Day 44: Questions for Reflection

1. How often do you allow others to take the lead?
2. How do you feel when someone else is in charge?
3. When did your instructions create a mess?
4. Which fears drive you to control things?
5. What experiences have you had with others' leading?
6. What bad things might happen if someone else is in control?
7. When would you like to invite another to take the lead?

AFFIRMATION 44:

I surrender my right to be in control.

Day 45:
Help, Lord!

"This poor man cried out, and the LORD heard him,
And saved him out of all his troubles" (Ps. 34:6).

Nature abhors a vacuum, and the ultimate vacuum seems to be a life adrift with no hand at the helm. We've seen countless lives dashed on the rocks. They may have arrived at the very shores of the Promised Land, only to suffer shipwreck within sight of home. Why? Careless inattention to duty. If anyone *was* at the helm, they must have fallen asleep. Someone *has* to be at the wheel.

Jesus, who spent a good deal of His time in the deliverance ministry, tells His disciples a disturbing story in Matthew 12:23-25. A man who had been under the control of a demon is fortunate enough to have the evil spirit cast out. Given the best of opportunities, the man blows the chance to regain possession of his life. Carelessness? Laziness? Ignorance? The Lord only tells us that the man makes no effort to fill the vacuum left by the demon. His tragedy begins with inaction. Does he feel competent to manage his own life? Oops! One might expect this twisted logic from a person who had suffered a demonic takeover.

**Jesus won, not only your battle
but your entire war.**

Meanwhile, the evicted spirit wanders around collecting friends and eventually returns to his old abode. Wow! The place looks good, clean, swept, and empty, so he moves back in with seven of his buddies, all worse than himself. The end of the man is *worse*, more than eight times worse! What went wrong? The man tried to run his own life. In case you think that *might* work, remember Adam and Eve, who demonstrated their inability to run their lives while living in a sinless world.

Jesus was warning you. Your enemy is incredibly strong, desperately determined, and widely experienced. Seeing how puny human beings appear in comparison, you may wonder how *anyone* escapes shipwreck. You certainly don't stand a chance one-on-one with the devil. The good news is Jesus has already won your battle. He fought because He knew you would be too weak to fight. He won, not only your battle but your entire war, but there's a catch. You knew it, didn't you?

The only way to obtain Jesus's victory is to surrender to Him. Once you make that decision, you are hidden in Christ, and His victory is yours. There's no other way to protect yourself. Surrender and you're safe under the shelter of God's wings. Fight your own battle, and you're fair game for the enemy. No one can run their own life, so choose carefully.

Day 45: Questions for Reflection

1. When did you give control of your life to another?
2. How pleased were you with their management?
3. What emotional baggage makes trusting God difficult?
4. In which areas does your life need new management?
5. In which areas are you doing a stellar job?
6. How competent are you to direct your affairs?
7. How capable a manager do you imagine God to be?

AFFIRMATION 45:

I ask God to take over my life.

DAY 46: JEHOVAH JIREH

"And Abraham called the name of the place, The-LORD-Will-Provide; as it is said to this day, 'In the Mount of the LORD it shall be provided'" Genesis 22:14).

There have been times when my trust was tested and found wanting, like the day my toddler chugged down Lysol. After I called Poison Control, I prayed. Oh, did I pray! My trembling lips spewed out a steady stream of desperate requests. "Please, God, don't let my baby die. Help me get this soapy water down him. Don't let his kidneys be damaged. Save his life."

I felt anything *but* relaxed. Two hours later, we found a ride to the Children's Hospital in Honolulu. By the time we arrived, my smiling baby had consumed the recommended twelve ounces of soapy water with no hint of nausea or vomiting. Bummers! The doctor sized up the small red marks around his lips.

"Nasty stuff, that Lysol. Sorry. We have to pump his stomach to make sure we get it all out." He reached for my baby. "We don't want him to suffer kidney damage."

Time stopped as I watched my precious son being carried through the white hospital door. I sat in the waiting room, stunned. How had I blown it so badly? I'd followed the rules: stored those cleaning supplies in a cabinet with a sliding lock six feet off the ground. I never imagined my four-year-old would stand on the bathroom counter to open the mysterious door while his brother watched from the floor. *Why, oh why hadn't I been more careful?*

When the door opened again, the doctor was carrying my red-faced toddler, eyes swollen from his battle. He looked as though he'd been beaten. His reproachful glance said clearly, "Why did you betray me?" As I held him to my heart, I felt like the world's worst mother. I hadn't been able to protect my child. I don't remember the long ride home. I was still numb. After my son was safely asleep in his crib, I went outside and cried.

God had come through beautifully. My son willingly drank a bottle of soapy water. The Lord sent us a ride to the hospital, and the baby suffered no kidney damage. All was well, yet I was undone. While my baby had been resting calmly in my arms, I had been fretting, begging, and fearing, instead of resting calmly in *my* Father's arms.

I used to believe God is good. Now I know. Years have passed since my son tasted the Lysol. He has a child of his own, and I'm sure the cleaning supplies are safely stored in his house. Now I pray for his soul. Fortunately, *I've* grown. I'm not fretting, begging, or fearing. I'm resting. God knows what He's doing, and His plans are perfect. He loves my son, so He's wooing him back to His arms.

Are you leaning on your Father? He hasn't failed you, even though you may think He has. Do you realize He never will? The failures are all human errors. I suspect you've done as many dumb things as I have. I locked the cleaning cabinet with a simple slider instead of a padlock, but the even more foolish thing was shaking with fear when I had already asked my Papa to take care of my oversight. I don't want you ever to feel the awful terror that consumed me. I want you to relax and trust God. He *will* provide for you as surely as He did for me.

Your Father hasn't failed you, even though you may think He has.

Day 46: Questions for Reflection

1. What exactly do you need? Make a list.
2. How many of these needs do you expect God to provide?
3. How relaxed do you feel about your unmet needs?
4. What needs has God provided in the past?
5. Have you shown God your list?
6. How confident are you that God will provide?
7. What would it take for you to relax in God's love?

AFFIRMATION 46:

I relax, knowing God will provide for me.

DAY 47: NOTICED BY GOD

"The heavens declare the glory of God; And the firmament shows His handiwork" (Ps. 19:1).

"Look at that," Marcy exclaimed. "Aren't they gorgeous? And to think the great God who created those constellations cares about me! It's awesome. Don't you love to camp under the stars?"

I rolled over in my sleeping bag, painfully aware of the sharp rock poking my hip, and mumbled an insincere assent. When *I* looked at the stars, I saw the same attributes of God Marcy perceived: limitless power, enormous creativity, and fantastic skill, but I didn't draw the same conclusions. Marcy felt reassured that her God was big enough to handle all difficulties; the God who flung the Pleiades into space could rescue one tiny human from the paltry problems of Earth. Hallelujah!

I don't know your reaction to the glories of space. Maybe you're lucky enough to feel Marcy's reassurance. When I looked at the scintillating expanse of black velvet studded with diamond stars, I was awed into insignificance. *Why should the God who rules the universe care about me?* As I pondered the faith-sapping question, I wondered if God might have lost track of me, a child who spoke of Christianity more glibly than she lived a selfless life.

God isn't out to get you.

Why did the same data produce such different reactions in my camping companion and me? As a child, Marcy was loved, praised, and accepted. She is quick to draw conclusions supporting her underlying feeling of being valuable, and she views the universe as friendly. I, on the other hand, was overlooked, criticized, and corrected, so I draw conclusions supporting my premise. The universe is hostile. What expectations did you derive from your upbringing? Were they nurturing or destructive?

The good news is that God loves and notices you every moment of every day. If you're like me, that realization may not take root in your battered heart for a while, but when you finally grasp what Marcy did, you'll know God loves you. Yes, you! He notices everything you do and even what you think. You're that important to Him, a fact which should wow you more than any constellation.

Pondering God's love may lead to an amazing conclusion: He isn't out to get you. He's not monitoring your life to catch you messing up and zap you. He has no desire to punish. What He *longs* to do is pour His richest blessings into you.

Wait a minute. What about calamity? When it does befall you, you can be sure of one thing: God's love allowed it, not to slap you down for failing, but to discipline and shape you so you won't fail again. God is not indifferent to you. He feels your pain. You're the apple of His eye.

Day 47: Questions for Reflection

---

1. How much acceptance and affirmation did you receive?
2. What do you expect from life?
3. How did your parents affect your relationship with God?
4. What does stargazing do for you?
5. How proud of you is God?
6. When you hear of a calamity, how do you feel?
7. What blessings have come from your calamities?

AFFIRMATION 47:

God is attentive to my needs.

Day 48:
Disaster Magnet

"Then Job arose, tore his robe, and shaved his head;
and he fell to the ground and worshiped. And he
said, 'Naked I came from my mother's womb,
And naked shall I return there. The LORD gave,
and the LORD has taken away. Blessed be the
name of the LORD" (Job 1:21).

I've known several people who were accident-prone, plagued by a continual rash of disasters. The first to convince me that *some* people's accidents were more than a string of bad luck was a woman who helped in the children's division of my church. First, she broke her elbow on the wall while turning a corner. By the time the elbow healed, she had zigzagged her finger with her new Singer, punching several needle holes through the nail. Before her finger healed, she sprinted across the patio to answer the phone, stubbed her toe on a tricycle, and fell, breaking her sternum on the corner of the cement steps. Double whammy! Bloody toe *and* broken breastbone!

My stepbrother rivaled this woman, falling off of motorcycles, out of the back of pickup trucks, and even out of cars. If he were helping to move a load of lumber, he was sure to be smacked in the head by a board. He routinely wore a bandage. Were his mishaps all accidental? The probability of one person suffering such a string of misfortunes is small; *really* small. I suspect both of these unfortunates felt a subconscious need to punish themselves.

I understand that mindset. I punished myself for years. If there was a drawing for a door prize, I never expected to win, and I never did. If, on the other hand, there was a drawing to see who would be assigned a distasteful task, I was sure I'd be chosen. Why? Because I felt guilty, I was convinced I deserved bad luck because I was such a *bad* person. Disliking the person who lives in your skin is rough, but projecting your dislike onto God is worse. You imagine *He* has targeted you for punishment, so you live in expectation of disaster.

Are you ready for the truth? No one is the special target of disaster. If anything, God has targeted us for blessings. What a relief! And what a difference! Once you realize God actually wishes you well and has a wonderful plan for your life, dismal outlooks evaporate like morning fog.

When you look for blessings, you find them. At a financial planning seminar, the facilitator announced that two watches would be given away as door prizes. With my new outlook, I instantly decided *I'm going to win one of them.* I did! Pretty good for a former Calamity Jane!

I'm not insinuating *all* problems are self-induced. They aren't. The average person may encounter drunk drivers, hailstorms, job layoffs, or any number of setbacks having little or nothing to do with mindset. But imagining oneself the target of adversity makes life's unavoidable difficulties harder. Besides, if you expect good rather than evil, you'll often find a benefit in the darkest circumstances. So why not choose to be the special target of blessings?

No one is the special target of disaster.

Day 48: Questions for Reflection

1. Why do some people experience so many disasters?
2. How do you process the misfortunes that befall you?
3. When were you the special target of trouble?
4. Why would a problem choose *you*?
5. On a scale of one to ten, how guilty do you feel?
6. How have you chosen to punish yourself?
7. What is God's part in your calamities?

AFFIRMATION 48:

I no longer think of myself as a victim.

Day 49: Phantom Fears

"Surely goodness and mercy shall follow me,
All the days of my life; And I shall dwell in the
house of the LORD Forever" (Ps. 23:6).

In a television commercial, a mother and daughter climb into the family van as the little girl tells her mom there's a monster in her bedroom. Mom is shaking her head in disbelief when the child's shaggy ogre charges the car. The announcer then assures the audience that purchasing the right van will protect them and their loved ones from all threats. *Ha!* No steel door ever stopped a thought, the stuff of which most monsters are built. Fleeting thoughts trigger your nervous system into high alert, causing great damage. If you need a little thought control, you're in good company.

You've heard Job's lament that the things he had tried so hard to avoid were the very calamities that befell him. There's a simple logic to the idea that you attract the things you fear. You walk in the direction you're looking, so focusing on the things you fear will sooner or later lead you to them. Take heart. If focusing on a certain trouble tends to cause that very problem, the opposite is also true. Focusing on God and His blessings moves you in a heavenly direction—away from Earth's petty difficulties and imminent dangers into a realm of love, joy, and peace.

Have you noticed that love, joy, and peace are diametrically opposed to fear? In fact, the apostle John tells us in his first epistle that mature, or perfect, love eliminates fear. "There is no fear in love; but perfect love casts out fear: because fear involves torment" (1 John 4:18).

You can be sure that if you're filled with love, joy, and peace, you're not focusing on your problems. Although they may still exist, they no longer hold your attention. You're riveted by something else, something with the potential to benefit, rather than destroy. Fear is a liar, promising protection but breeding paralysis. Although you may secretly chuckle at the plight of the claustrophobic, you also may harbor a phobia. In your heart of hearts, would you like to sing, dance, draw, paint, or act? Why don't you? The monster!

Fear is a thief as well as a liar. He robs you of your dreams with poisonous falsehoods and dastardly rumors, immobilizing your resolve. Are you sick of his lies? Ignore them and they evaporate. As for those that are harder to shake, unmask them and deny them. That's your heritage as a child of the King. Won't you join me in bold fearlessness? Who knows? If we stop entertaining fear, the things we *want* may overtake us. I'm counting on it.

Fear is a liar, promising protection but breeding paralysis.

Day 49: Questions for Reflection

1. What is your worst fear?
2. How long have you been plagued by this "monster?"
3. How has this concern benefited you?
4. What would happen if you stopped being afraid?
5. Which dreams could you pursue?
6. Do you want to keep *some* of your fears?
7. When would you like to abandon the others?

AFFIRMATION 49:

The things I feared are phantoms.

Day 50:
Canceling Red Alert

"For I, the LORD your God, will hold your right hand, saying to you, 'Fear not, I will help you'" (Isa. 41:13).

What could be more peaceful than a babe asleep in Mother's arms, mouth agape, eyes gently closed? Cuddled to his mother's heart, he sleeps soundly, though his head may droop until the slight neck seems bent at an excruciating angle. He is at peace. The baby sleeps because he is fearless. Mother is watching, and she would lay down her life to protect him. He knows this, and because he trusts her, his world is safe. Eventually, he will build a confident life on the foundation of the security he enjoyed in her arms.

Some of us didn't experience that idyllic scene. We weren't secure as children, and we don't feel safe as adults. Programmed to survive, all human beings experience a disconcerting surge of adrenaline when danger threatens, but perceptions of danger vary greatly from one individual to the next. Some of us have our hazard detectors set to sensitive, so sensitive that we perceive peril in the most secure circumstances. Life is a vigil, guard duty with no relief.

While still in the womb, I was subjected to screaming matches between my parents. The cocktail of emergency-response chemicals coursing through my mother's bloodstream took its toll on me, as did the bruises I sustained in the resultant melees. My prenatal traumas predisposed me to a self-protective vigilance, which increased my chances of survival in the hostile environment into which I was born.

I hope your story is different, but if the only traumas you experienced were caustic words, they are every bit as damaging.

You are not alone. You have never been alone. God was there when you were born.

Long after I had grown and my parents were dead, I still kept watch. My psyche was set on red alert, and I was exhausted. Had a real foe confronted me, I could have anticipated his moves, planned my strategy, and attacked or retreated. I, however, was stalked by the ghost of past traumas, tormented by shrieks in the wasteland of my subconscious. If you've identified with this, your nerves may be frayed and your fleeting joys darkened. A foreboding of disaster hangs over a tormented life.

If you have no memory of a warm parental nest, you may feel alone and exposed, but your feelings are inaccurate. You are *not* alone. You have *never* been alone. God was there when you were born, loving and protecting you, and He still holds you in his arms today. Only after you let yourself *feel* those everlasting arms will you experience the peace you missed as a child and know you are safe. *Whew!* Once you get there, take a long nap, cuddled up to your heavenly Father's heart.

Day 50: Questions for Reflection

1. How peaceful was your prenatal experience?
2. What are your memories of a safe parental nest?
3. Who nurtured and protected you in infancy?
4. What dangers threatened your early days?
5. How secure do you feel today?
6. Where do you go to find peace and rest?
7. Have you found your heavenly Father's arms?

AFFIRMATION 50:

I release the strain of protecting myself.

Day 51:
My Father's Arms

"The eternal God is your refuge, And underneath are the everlasting arms" (Deut. 33:27).

Overcoming fear is easy. You've all done it, and even helped someone else do it. If a toddler starts screaming when approached by a dog, you pick the baby up and cuddle him. "There, there. It's all right. That's just old Rover. He won't hurt you. See, you can pet him."

Once the tot is safe in your arms, you slowly lower him to Rover's height. A tentative hand stretches toward the soft fur. The child may recoil at the sight of Rover's pointy teeth, but as the dog's warm tongue caresses his hand, the toddler relaxes. The animal is friendly. Within minutes, the child is rolling on the floor with Rover, giggling.

What happened? Rover didn't change. As the toddler acquired additional information, *he* changed. His perception of Rover is now based on reality rather than conjecture. His experience leaves him feeling calm, confident, and even playful in the canine's presence. A terrifying moment has been transformed by the security of the strong arms holding him.

When you find yourself in an alarming situation, do you long for someone bigger and stronger to pick you up and lift you to safety? God, in His great mercy, gave me such a person when I was a child. He was a big man, a car mechanic, and I *knew* in the marrow of my baby bones he loved me. Every time he walked by my playpen, he made a fist and jokingly threatened, "I'm going to bop you."

One day, when he stepped into the room, I screeched, "Bopoo! Bopoo!" The moniker stuck.

When I got a little older, I was able to voice my request more eloquently. "Bopoo, take her and keep her."

He always picked me up. I wished that he would never put me down. Then we moved away from Ohio and his Pure Oil Gas Station. I was twelve years old the summer we returned, too big to pick up, but my Bopoo didn't care. He picked me up anyway. Remembering how much I needed his arms brings tears to my eyes today. When we moved away two years later, I was disconsolate. How would I survive without Bopoo?

A few years later, reading the end of Deuteronomy, I realized how disheartened the Israelites must have felt at the prospect of losing Moses, the grand old man who had led them for forty years through the desert. His arms had lifted the rod that divided the Red Sea so they could escape the Egyptian army. Those arms, uplifted to God, had brought victory when Joshua fought the Amalekites. They had carried the Ten Commandments down from Mount Sinai and lifted the brass serpent, bringing healing in the wilderness to the grumblers who were dying of snake bites. Now, he must leave them, but not without the words of consolation in today's scripture. The invisible God had been their refuge all along, and His arms would always be ready to receive them.

Today's scripture is sweeter than a hot fudge sundae. Did you catch the depth of those words? *Someone* loves you; Someone so big, He'll always be able to pick you up. You are *safe!* God sent a humble mechanic into my love-starved life to teach me to trust those arms that never grow weary. The good news is He will hold you, too. Ask Him to pick you up and keep you forever, and He will.

Someone loves you; Someone so big, He'll always be able to pick you up.

Day 51: Questions for Reflection

1. Who picked you up when you were little?
2. How has that experience helped you overcome anxiety?
3. Which concerns still trouble you?
4. What means have you tried to overcome them?
5. When do you feel safe?
6. What do you do when you're afraid?
7. How do you feel when you read God wants to hold you?

AFFIRMATION 51:

I take shelter in God's arms.

Day 52:
Real Protection

"Your eyes saw my substance, being yet unformed.
And in Your book they all were written, The days
fashioned for me, When as yet there were
none of them" (Ps. 139:16).

I suspect each one of us is afraid of something. What is it for you? Germs? Thunderstorms? Someone else's driving? The last one was big for me. My mother loved big cars with V-8 engines and glass-pack mufflers. When a stranger grabbed her door handle at a stoplight, she floored the accelerator and rolled the agent assigned to repossess her car across a Los Angeles intersection. He caught up with her on the Grapevine, but pull her over? Not my mother! She outran him handily.

My drunken father's driving was ever scarier. When he topped a hundred miles an hour in a fit of rage on the freeway, I had a great opportunity to learn fervent prayer. Sudden stops proved even worse. My front teeth shattered when they hit the metal strip on the back of the driver's seat, which meant I never dared to smile for a school photograph again.

If we were sitting around my kitchen table, I'm sure each of you could share a similar story. Either you have been in a traffic accident or a natural disaster, or barely missed one. You're not sure why you didn't die that day. You may have walked away without a scratch or with minor abrasions, wondering why you were still alive. Not everyone is so lucky. My brother broke his neck when he was thrown from his car, but he did survive. He had not fulfilled the days allotted to him.

You and I were born with an expiration date, but it's not stamped on the bottom of our feet. It's written in God's book. He knew how many days He'd fashioned for you before you were born. Sometimes I wonder whether that number is a guarantee of how long we'll live or simply our potential, which we can cut short by bad choices. Either way, God knew about our decisions before He wrote down the date.

My father died in his fifties from alcohol abuse, and my mother passed in her sixties from smoking. Doctors say cancer killed them. No, the lifestyles they chose brought them to their expiration dates far too soon. My great-grandmother, who depended on God rather than alcohol or nicotine, died in her late nineties.

God will have one question for you. What did you do with the talents I gave you?

Now we come to you and how much you trust God to protect you. You're alive today because God wants you here on Earth at this moment. You have a purpose you haven't yet accomplished. You may have been assigned an Earth-shaking mission like finding a cure for cancer, or you may have been appointed a seemingly small task like raising an abandoned grandchild, caring for a baby with Down Syndrome, or supporting a spouse with Alzheimer's.

What seems small here will look quite different in eternity. Imagine the reward waiting for Jochebed, the slave mother who hid baby Moses in a basket on the Nile, or Hannah, the barren woman who vowed to give her child to God and was rewarded with Samuel. What honor is reserved for Mary, the teenager who nursed the baby Jesus? When you meet God, He will have one question, the question Jesus highlighted in the parable of the talents: "What did you do with the talents I gave you?"

You *can't* do much with your talents while your energy is dedicated to self-protection, even on a subconscious level. Once you feel safe, you can use your energy to build God's kingdom. Are you ready to grow, blossom, and bear fruit? The world is waiting for what you alone can offer.

Day 52: Questions for Reflection

1. In which areas can you protect yourself?
2. In which areas do you feel vulnerable?
3. What security problems have you encountered?
4. When were you helpless to save yourself?
5. When were you inexplicably rescued?
6. Why do you believe God can save you?
7. What do you know about your ability to protect yourself?

AFFIRMATION 52:

I am learning to trust God's protection.

Day 53:
Learning to Trust

"He shall call upon Me, and I will answer him; I will be
with him in trouble; I will deliver him and honor him"
(Ps. 91:15).

If you're like me, you've had dozens, or even hundreds, of close calls when you were seconds from death. Sometimes you were oblivious to the danger until it had passed. I had such an experience last week following a rare opportunity to meet with a friend who lives in the next town. Her husband dropped her off at my house.

I had agreed to take her to work, well, *close* to work, as my friend works at a shelter for battered women, whose location is a closely-guarded secret. After practicing a duet and hiking down to the river, we got into my car. As I drove, we laughed and talked until she directed me to turn off the main road into a small parking lot.

After she got out of the car, I stared across the four lanes of traffic, looking for an opening to make a left turn. A space appeared... or so I thought. Squinting against the lowering sun, I swung across the two lanes closest to me, narrowly evading a huge dinosaur of a car that whooshed past me out of nowhere, missing me by seconds. *Whew!*

When my heart stopped racing, I thanked God for saving my life. I could easily have died. The crisis was over before I realized I was in danger, and I was safe. *Again!* I've driven for sixty years without suffering more than a minor fender bender. Why? Yes, I'm cautious. My husband would call me *overly* cautious. But I don't credit my survival to my cautious driving.

Do you number your days, or do you forget they're limited?

Life seems especially sweet after such an episode. I praised God all the way home while I meditated on several suddenly vital questions. *Why am I here? What am I supposed to be doing? Am I accomplishing my earthly mission?* Pondering these questions is good. As Moses stated so eloquently: "So teach us to number our days, that we may gain a heart of wisdom" *(Ps. 90:12).*

Do you number your days, or do you forget they're limited? While you're counting, remember the final tally is in God's hands. You'll be here until the days He has appointed for you have been completed. In the meantime, you can enjoy the time He's allotted and make each day productive. To do that, you'll have to stop worrying.

Jesus declared His purpose in John 10:10: "I have come that they may have life, and that they may have it more abundantly."

Abundant life sounds good—really good! If you're not enjoying an abundant life now, I suggest you check in with those questions I was pondering. Why are you here? What are you supposed to be doing? Are you accomplishing your unique mission? Chances are, you will have abundant energy to devote to your calling once you learn to trust God and stop protecting yourself.

Day 53: Questions for Reflection

1. When have you survived a near-death experience?
2. To what do you credit your survival?
3. Do you think of God as on your side or out to get you?
4. Why do some people live through tragedies while others die?
5. How abundant is your life?
6. When would you like to live more abundantly?
7. What keeps you from trusting God's protection?

AFFIRMATION 53:

God's Secret Service surrounds me.

Day 54:
The Good Side of Fear

"Oh fear the LORD, you His saints! There is no
want to those who fear Him" (Ps. 34:9).

Fear is universal. We can experience that dread emotion from before
the day we're born. I'm not talking about the fear of bright lights,
cold air in the delivery room, or squeezing through the birth canal.
I'm talking about a terror of destruction. After months of listening
to brawls between my parents, I suddenly emerged into the midst
of their war zone, defenseless. Fear crippled me.

For years, I dressed in layers, afraid of feeling too hot or cold.
I worked twelve-hour days to avoid failing to please everyone. I
smiled at people who insulted me, cried in private, and rarely
confronted even the most atrocious behavior. The classic target
for bullies, I was speechless in the face of abuse, not realizing God
hadn't created me to be a doormat.

To my amazement, the Bible lists *one* single, legitimate object of
fear: God Himself. Reread today's scripture. Some modern trans-
lations prefer "reverence" to "fear," but the Hebrew word for fear in
this verse, according to the lexical aids to the Old Testament in the
Hebrew Greek Study Bible, has two primary meanings. The first
is the emotional and intellectual anticipation of harm. The second
is a very positive feeling of awe or reverence for God.

The Greek word for "fear" in the New Testament is "phobos,"
the root word for phobia, a panic-attack level of terror, which Israel

experienced when God spoke to them from Mount Sinai. Hearing His voice thunder through the lightning and fire, the people were convinced they were about to die. Their God was setting the very rocks ablaze! Falling on their faces, they begged Moses to act as a go-between.

Why did God scare them? And why does He want you to fear him? He knows humans were created to fear or worship God. When they do, the good, clean, wholesome fear of the Lord immunizes them against the evil, dirty, unwholesome fear of anything else. The Bible's many "fear nots" cover everything from enemy soldiers to death.

In Psalm 27:1, we read: "The LORD is my light and my salvation; Whom shall I fear? The LORD is the strength of my life; Of whom shall I be afraid?"

Excellent question! If you are a child of the Almighty, whose presence sets men's hearts quaking, you have nothing to fear, not even the ultimate enemy: death. The apostle Paul was looking forward to the day when he would lay aside his earthly tent and go to live with God.

One thing is as sure as tomorrow's sunrise: your fears did not come from the Lord. "For God has not given us a spirit of fear, but of power and of love and of a sound mind" (2 Tim. 1:7).

God has given you a mind capable of making wise decisions and the power to make them! Focus your fear on the only One worthy of worship, and use your willpower to fear nothing else. Nothing besides God is worthy of your worship.

If you are a child of the Almighty, you have nothing to fear, not even death.

Day 54: Questions for Reflection

1. What is your worst fear?
2. How much do you fear God?
3. How does fear frustrate God's plan for you?
4. When did you thank God for a sound mind?
5. What has your power of choice accomplished?
6. What would you like to choose?
7. How would your life change if you feared only God?

AFFIRMATION 54:

I fear only God.

Day 55:
The Bad Side of Fear

"Be strong and of good courage, do not fear
or be afraid of them; for the LORD your God,
He is the One who goes with you. He will not
leave you nor forsake you" (Deut. 31:6).

Even Christians who profess confidence in God's ability to protect them may have to actively reject fear. When danger threatens, we instinctively try to defend ourselves or flee. Once the adrenaline is pumping, you and I have a hard time hearing God's voice. We *want* to hear Him. We really do. We've indulged our fight-or-flight tendencies long enough to know we're not very good at protecting ourselves.

I have to admit I sometimes fail to reject fear and trust God. One such occasion concerned my fifth-period high school Spanish class. During the last period of the day, teenagers focus more on the clock than on the lesson. This group was a miserable mixture of serious scholars and goof-offs. Among the latter was a handsome eighteen-year-old I'll call Ted. Although several girls were interested in helping Ted raise his grade, his only interest seemed to be sleeping. When I wouldn't give him a pass to the nurse's office, which boasted a bed, he lay his head on the desk and dozed.

Ted hadn't turned in an assignment for two months when he informed me he wouldn't be allowed to play in the state championship football game the next evening if I gave him an "F" in Spanish.

Besides, he needed the credit to graduate in a few months. As Ted roused himself from his customary nap that day, I heard him mutter something which included the word "kill."

As I opened my eyes the next morning, I realized he had said, "I'm going to kill you."

Recent reports of students murdering teachers flashed through my mind. Ted was the classic disgruntled misfit from an alternative school who took medication to control his moods, a time-release drug which had worn off by fifth period. As this information settled into my bones, I started to shake. Did I thank God for the situation and put Ted into His capable hands? No. I tried to figure out a way to avoid being shot! Hadn't the school just added a resource officer because of a failed shooting?

I went to school an hour early and emailed Ted's counselor, his caseworker, and the vice principal. Soon, Ted sauntered in, a paper in his hand. *Okay, good. No gun in sight.* Response to my emails had been immediate. His special education caseworker arrived moments later, apologetic at having failed to notice his grade, which she should have been monitoring.

Rest in Father's arms, even while taking prudent, self-protective measures.

When the dust settled, Ted had been re-enrolled in the alternative school, where he could graduate without Spanish credit, and he *would* be eligible to play in the all-important football game that evening. The emergency was over, but as my first-period students filed in, my left eye began to pulsate. By the time the throbbing stopped, I was seeing flashes of light whenever I turned my head. *You're all right. Take a deep breath. Sit down.* Having weathered a recent retinal tear, I recognized the seriousness of my symptoms. Yes, I had been a *little* stressed.

You'd like to *think* you trust God to protect you, but when danger threatens, you may discover you're still learning. Do you let your imagination dredge up the worst-case scenario? (Ted admitted he had said, "I'm going to kill you," but he claimed he was joking with the girl who had just sprinkled water on his face to awaken him.)

If there's a lesson here, that lesson is to rest in Father's arms, even while taking prudent, self-protective measures. As my SCUBA instructor admonished, "After you panic, regain control and follow your training." In this case, your training is to call upon God, your spiritual 911, and trust He'll show up in time. He always does.

Day 55: Questions for Reflection

1. What frightens you?
2. How do you deal with your fears?
3. When did you fail to save yourself?
4. When did God protect you?
5. How many times has God rescued you?
6. What would help you trust God's protection?
7. How would a fearless life be different?

AFFIRMATION 55:

I release the ungodly fears that have ruled me.

Day 56:
Unhealthy Isolation

"And the LORD God said, 'It is not good that man should be alone; I will make him a helper comparable to him'" (Gen. 2:18).

Biologists refer to humans as social animals, meaning our species prefers to live in groups. Groups are more than a preference. We *need* social interaction. Isolation is so painful that solitary confinement is reserved as the direst punishment for the incorrigible. The devastating effect of this penalty was pressed home to me when the inmate I was visiting at the women's prison on Oahu attempted suicide soon after being assigned to solitary confinement. God was right when He said man should not be alone. That same day, He fashioned a woman.

Given our widely acknowledged social needs, you would think instruction in the skills needed to develop relationships would be a top priority in our homes and schools. If such a class was ever offered, I missed it, and I suspect you did too. Some of us really needed those lessons. Have you noticed people who don't relate well to others? They may seem untouchable because of the walls they've built to protect themselves. That was me.

I once read a poster stating: "The highest fences we climb are those we build within our minds." Hmmm. The walls protecting your delicate ego from those who demand too much from you also filter out friends who fail to meet your stringent criteria. You and I have a tendency to treat others the way we've been treated. Hurt people hurt people, and the wounded are naturally guarded, which makes getting the companionship you and I crave a challenge.

Earning a high school diploma involved my attending a score of schools in three states. I can still feel the agony of walking into the cafeteria on my first day in a new school. Alone in a crowd, I watched smiling faces greeting friends they'd known since Kindergarten while I searched desperately for a place to hide. A hole in the floor would have been ideal, but the average cafeteria had foolishly neglected to provide one. So, I sat in the corner, eyes on my food, avoiding the gaze of the elite who had friends. In case you're wondering, no, the second day *wasn't* easier. Knowing I'd be off to the next school before the year was over, I rarely reached out to my peers.

But my isolation was eclipsed by the pain of self-rejection. My deepest wound was self-inflicted! Having been told since infancy that I was clumsy, unattractive, and devoid of common sense, I despised myself, imagining my only hope of becoming socially acceptable lay in hiding who I was. For my entire youth, I lived a hypocrite's hell, striving to conform to the desires of others, berating myself for every faux pas, and hating my ineptitude.

You may not have lacked friends, but even those with lifelong buddies have been disappointed. You may turn to God, hoping He'll accept you into His group, but wonder if He will. Or you may berate God for making you a loser. The Bible says Jesus is the Friend of sinners. Why does He seem distant? Those walls you've built? He respects them.

You don't need to isolate.
You have nothing to hide.

The Bible says God loved Abraham, Isaac, and Jacob, even though they had done some sleazy things. Both Abraham and Isaac handed their wives over to foreign kings to save their skins. Jacob lied to his father to defraud his brother. If God could love men like that, He can love you. He can even love me, a grown-up child others labeled clumsy, ugly, and devoid of common sense. What labels did people pin on you? Did you believe them and add more of your own?

The truth that God loves you exactly the way He made you should settle the matter. You don't need to isolate. You have nothing to hide. Your trust in God, yourself, and your fellow man may not arrive in one big chocolate-covered lump. You may need time to take down your walls. God put his wrecking ball into storage after Jericho. He's waiting for *you* to take down those walls and invite Him in. Bonus? He'll bring His friends with Him.

Day 56: Questions for Reflection

1. On a scale of one to ten, how isolated do you feel?
2. Do you feel more isolated from yourself, God, or others?
3. How do you make friends?
4. What blocks healthy relationships?
5. Why do you need protective walls?
6. How could you escape from your fortress?
7. Who are you expecting to rescue you?

AFFIRMATION 56:

Isolation is painful and unhealthy.

Day 57:
Relationships

"A man who has friends must himself be friendly,
but there is a friend who sticks closer than a brother"
(Prov. 18:24).

Do you consider yourself an exception to the first line of John Donne's poem: "No man is an island, entire of itself?"

The words seem true for people warmly enmeshed with friends and family, but you may feel alone. Have you coped by erecting an invisible shield? The shield doesn't work—not really. You feel clever in your safe world, but you also feel empty. My husband was fond of saying there are only three things in the universe: people, things, and ideas. Once you exclude people, you're left with only things and ideas.

Imagine God surveying His world on the morning of the sixth day of creation. Earth brimmed with pine, cedar, and oak trees, slippery trout and salmon, and colorful peacocks. His mind over-flowed with ideas which became reality the moment He spoke them, filling the land with an astounding array of animals. His work was good, He decided, but incomplete. The world needed people. After He had created a pair of humans capable of relating to Him, His creation, and each other, He inspected his handiwork again and decreed it *very* good.

God knew His world needed people. Maybe you, like me, thought your world could get by without them. Like a shipwrecked sailor washed up on a deserted island, did you determine to survive alone? You may manage a sort of physical existence, but life seems void.

What good is your cure for arthritis if no one knows about it? Why think great thoughts which never meet the test of other minds? Self-preservation is a narrow goal. And why survive? A man wrapped up in himself is a small package. The solitary human is a pitiable creature: crippled, undeveloped, and unaware of his faults.

Trying to live a solitary life is akin to sinking a ship to eliminate the wood-boring worms.

Trying to live a solitary life is akin to sinking a ship to eliminate the wood-boring worms. The cost is horrendous and the reward minuscule. The gnawing pain of isolation is worse than the momentary pangs of betrayal or abandonment. The Creator's purpose cannot be foiled. As the wise man notes: "There are many plans in a man's heart; Nevertheless, the LORD's counsel that will stand" (Prov. 19:21).

Any idea you have that is contrary to God's will doesn't amount to a sandcastle in a tsunami. Sooner or later, your dream of self-sufficiency will blow away in the wind, if the tides of life don't erase it first. God knows what you need. If He created this world and filled His Earth with people in meaningful relationships, the best you can do is embrace His perfect plan.

Day 57: Questions for Reflection

---

1. Rank people, things, and ideas in importance.
2. Which of the three has caused you the most pain?
3. How do you cope with emotional firestorms?
4. What good has resulted from painful experiences?
5. When have you excluded others to protect yourself?
6. Which is more painful, isolation or a relationship?
7. What rewards have you gained from a solitary life?

AFFIRMATION 57:

God created me to relate to others.

Day 58: Healthy Relationships

"A friend loves at all times,
And a brother is born for adversity"
(Prov. 17:17).

As human beings, we have the awesome privilege of making decisions. Ancestors, culture, and experience may influence us, but our destinies are not determined by factors over which we have no control. We are more than a bundle of instincts. Unlike animals, we are children of God, endowed with the kingly power of reason and the ability to imagine and initiate change.

Viktor Frankl, an Austrian psychiatrist and Holocaust survivor, was astounded at the selfless behavior he observed in Nazi death camps. While some starving inmates isolated themselves and hoarded their meager stores of food, others gave their rations to those who were weaker, making the decision to live their finest hours in hideous circumstances.

Stepping out of familiar, self-protective habits takes courage, but I've seen a gorilla accomplish it. I was fascinated by a television documentary which showed a silverback known as the Shopping Mall Gorilla. He had been on display in the B & I shopping mall in Tacoma, Washington, for twenty-seven years until a public outcry prevailed. Arrangements were made for the 500-pound primate, named Ivan in a children's book, to live the rest of his days in an idyllic setting: Zoo Atlanta, where a lush jungle habitat had been designed to simulate a natural environment.

The gorilla's benefactors hoisted his cage into the new setting and stepped back to videotape his reaction. What did he do? Nothing! His sense of security was wrapped up in the cage, his only defense against fingers poked at him. After three days of furtive glances at his new surroundings, he mustered the courage to take a single step outside. Twenty seconds later, he raced back. A week later, he was able to spend extended periods of time outside, but still returned to the cage when frightened. Only after his positive, out-of-cage experiences outweighed his former conditioning were his benefactors able to remove the cage.

I cried as I watched. That gorilla was courageous. I rooted for him: *Go on. Get out there. You'll make it.* His new habitat included others of his kind, but having lived alone, he had no social skills. Learning the lessons of relationships in midlife wasn't easy. As I watched, I had no doubt he should brave the trauma of adapting to a better life. How exciting to see him become all that a gorilla was created to be. *Bravo! Good job! You succeeded!*

The tears I shed as I watched were more for myself than the gorilla. I had been the one to lock myself in the cage. Like Linus in the Charlie Brown cartoons, I had held onto my security blanket. Not willing to be outdone by an ape, I decided to reclaim my dreams. What dreams have you abandoned? God will give you the courage to heal, so you can become all He created you to be. The apostle Paul said in Philippians 4:13: "I can do all things through Christ who strengthens me."

Do you believe Christ will give you the strength to step out of your cage? Yes, you do? Congratulations! The question is when. The moment you are willing to receive His power, resolution will grip your weakened will. You will leave your cage behind, brave the trauma of learning to relate, and join me in nurturing healthy friendships. They count more than money or fame.

God will give you the courage to heal, so you can become all He created you to be.

Day 58: Questions for Reflection

1. When did you first choose to isolate?
2. What degree of isolation feels comfortable?
3. How fulfilling is your isolation?
4. What dreams sustain you?
5. What keeps you from claiming those dreams?
6. What does "I can do all things through Christ" mean?
7. When will you begin living your preferred lifestyle?

AFFIRMATION 58:

The pain of isolation is intense.

Day 59:
Costly Relationships

"A new commandment I give you, that you love one another; as I have loved you, that you also love one another" (John 13:34).

God has interesting ways to ambush you and me. When we least expect Him, He shakes the foundations of our cherished beliefs. I'm sure He has surprised you from time to time, just as He did me one hot summer day. Weary from wandering through Glacier National Park's museum, I flopped onto a hard bench in a darkened room to watch a documentary. What I saw that afternoon changed my life.

The black-and-white film chronicled the life of a Native American, the last of the Yahi Indians, a group of Yana who lived on Mill Creek around Oroville, California. The white men named him Ishi. Ishi's father had been killed in a village massacre when he was a boy, but he and his mother had escaped by jumping into the river. They had lived with forty fugitives hidden in the foothills, hunting with bows and arrows, skinning deer, and fashioning clothing from the hides.

Settlers assumed the "Mill Creek Indians" were all gone until 1908, when a group of power company surveyors stumbled on a Native American man fishing in the creek. The next day, they found a tiny village, home to the last four survivors. A young woman fled with an old man, and neither was ever seen again. An old woman, too sick to move, watched as the surveyors looted the village, taking the food as well as the hunting and fishing supplies. Ishi returned to discover his mother alone and dying. Three years after he sang her death song, he made a decision whose audacity staggers me.

On August 29, 1911, Ishi stepped out of the woods and approached a white man. The astounded rancher motioned a clear message: go back into the woods. The savage stood his ground. Terrified, the rancher called the authorities, and the sheriff put the "wild man" in the local jail. Alfred Kroeber and T.T. Waterman, professors of anthropology at the University of California, located in Berkeley, soon became Ishi's guardians. For five years, they studied his language and culture while helping him adapt to modern life. The trauma of stepping from an ancient culture into twentieth-century America was the equivalent of waking up on a space station.

Ishi was right.
The pain of relationship is worth the price.

Although Ishi managed a brave smile when they took his picture in a suit and tie, I'm sure he found the clothing uncomfortable. I can't imagine he was favorably impressed with the white man's world. His refusal of a woman's offer to have his child so his line would not die out speaks volumes. Yet, I am also sure Ishi never regretted his decision. He preferred being studied as a curiosity to speaking only to the wind. I applaud his courage in approaching a group he knew only as thieves and murderers. Sadly, he died five years later from tuberculosis, a white man's disease.

I brushed away a tear as Ishi's face faded from the screen. When the lights came on in that little room at Glacier National Park, I became aware of the hard plastic bench beneath me. My bottom was sore, but not as sore as my soul. I'd experienced a pain similar to Ishi's, but I'd played the coward, hiding for fear of being hurt. Ishi was right. The pain of a relationship is worth the price. Have you embraced that truth, or are you still hiding?

Day 59: Questions for Reflection

1. Who has isolated you?
2. Why have you isolated yourself?
3. Is isolation brave, cowardly, or both?
4. If you were Ishi, what would you have done?
5. What happens if you invite more people into your life?
6. How much do relationships cost?
7. What benefits have you gained from friends?

AFFIRMATION 59:

I choose to nurture healthy relationships.

Day 60:
God Is Real

"Be still and know that I am God; I will be exalted among the nations, I will be exalted in the earth" (Ps. 46:10)!

I hope you were blessed with a Christian home and parents who loved the Lord and raised you to rely on Him. My husband's mother told him about God when he was three years old. He was so impressed, he said, "Well, God, if You're so big, I'd like to meet you."

BAM! God revealed Himself to a little boy. My husband never forgot the experience, though he could never articulate what he'd seen. His response had been immediate, "Okay, I'm yours. I'll be whatever you want." He remained true to his word for the rest of his life.

My experience was quite different. My mother seemed to hope God might be a myth, but I managed to ascertain two facts before I went to Kindergarten: one, God was up there somewhere, and two, I could talk to him. I'm not sure where I got those ideas. No one I knew went to church, and the only prayer I heard was a lengthy grace over rare holiday meals at my great-grandmother's house. Yet, I began to pray when I was little, especially when my heart was broken.

A turning point in my spiritual journey happened the day a neighbor, talking with my mother over the back fence, picked a few tiny wildflowers and handed me the bouquet. The blossoms wilted soon after I put them in my room. Dismayed, I showed them to my mother.

"You killed them. They needed to be put in water," she scolded.

Conscience-stricken, I fled to my room, got down on my knees, and implored God to revive my precious posies. Then I filled the cap of a fountain pen with water, put the droopy blooms in the tiny receptacle, and clipped it to a dress in my darkened closet. The next morning, when I opened the closet door to find the fragile flowers revived, I knew beyond all doubt—God was real! Not only that, but He had heard and answered a child's prayer.

Thirty years later, my brother's accident showed me how instinctively those who don't want to believe God exists cry out to Him when disaster strikes. Weeks after my father's death, my brother took to the road in his new Volvo with a girlfriend at the wheel and a bottle of wine in the front seat. The joy ride ended when she hit a dirt embankment at fifty miles an hour. They both flew out of the car.

John saw her lying in the road but couldn't move. His neck was broken, his girlfriend dead. When my mother told me there was no sense flying to see him because John was in intensive care with limited visiting hours, I promised to pray for him. "I've been doing some of that myself," she admitted without embarrassment.

My skeptical mother praying? I suspect we *all* pray when the chips are down because somewhere deep inside, when we are still, we *know* God is real.

God invites you to taste and see because that may be the only way you can be sure He's real.

"This poor man cried out, and the LORD heard him, And saved him out of all his troubles. The angel of the LORD encamps all around those who fear him, and delivers them. Oh, taste and see that the LORD is good; Blessed is the man who trusts in Him" (Ps. 34:6-8).

God invites you to taste and see because only by experiencing Him can you be sure He's real. Like an ice-cream shop that offers a taste spoon, the God of the universe invites you to partake of His goodness. The risen Christ invited Thomas to put his finger into the wounds of the nails so he could believe. In the same way, God invites you to bring Him into the realm of your experience. If you're anything like my husband, one taste and you won't be satisfied with anything else.

Day 60: Questions for Reflection

1. What did you learn about God from your parents?
2. When did you begin to suspect God was real?
3. How did those around you react to questions about God?
4. Why do you believe God exists?
5. How loving is the God of your imagination?
6. How has God made all things work together for your good?
7. When have God's angels intervened in your life?

AFFIRMATION 60:

God is real.

Day 61:
A Great Big God

"Have you not known? Have you not heard? The everlasting God, the LORD, the Creator of the ends of the earth, Neither faints nor is weary. His understanding is unsearchable" (Isa. 40:28).

The cubicle of the modern corporate world allows people to work in close proximity, yet partitioned off from one another. The idea of separation isn't new. In the ancient world, entire cities were partitioned off, surrounded by thick walls with massive gates that could be bolted against intruders. Some walls were broad enough to accommodate houses; others boasted roads. A strong wall provided protection. The taller the wall, the better it withstood ladders thrust against the sides or flaming missiles lobbed over the top. The thicker the wall, the better it resisted the battering ram. The ancients considered a good wall well worth their time and effort.

The Bible assures you Jesus is the Friend of sinners, so why does He seem distant? He respects those walls you've built. Don't berate yourself for being a loser or reproach God for the way He created you. *I'm such a dork. No wonder no one likes me. I'm not even sure God cares about me. Where is He, anyway?* He's outside your wall.

Tear down your wall. God's been waiting to wash away your shame.

The next time you wonder whether God *really* loves *you*, remember that God loved King David, calling him a man after His own heart. Do you remember David? Yes, he killed Goliath, but he also got another man's wife pregnant while her husband, Uriah, was out fighting in David's war. Then he had Uriah killed to cover up his sin. If God could love David, He can love you.

Once you believe God loves you, you burst free from the need to isolate. There's no longer anything to hide. After his double, deadly sins of adultery and murder, David wrote Psalm 51, his song of repentance, which is distributed in the most widely read book of all time. Are you as free of shame? Maybe you're ready to remove your mask, step out of your cubicle, and tear down your wall. God's been waiting to wash away your shame.

Day 61: Questions for Reflection

1. Did you grow up emotionally open or insulated?
2. Which circumstances make you feel vulnerable?
3. What barriers have you erected for protection?
4. What happens when you invite others into your fortress?
5. How would you feel if you saw God peeking over your walls?
6. What kind of life are you living inside your walls?
7. Where is God today in relation to your defense system?

AFFIRMATION 61:

God is bigger than my barriers.

Day 62:
Embracing Hope

"Now may the God of hope fill you with all joy and peace in believing, that you may abound in hope by the power of the Holy Spirit" (Rom. 15:13).

The apostle Paul boldly asserts that hope is the heritage of the believer. We're encouraged to *abound* in hope. How have you been doing with abundance? I blush to admit there have been times when I would have been hard-pressed to produce a pinch of hope, much less an abundance. By the age of thirteen, my store had dwindled to zero.

The problem was not my family's gypsy lifestyle of moving from state to state, often in the middle of the school year. Had I been more of an extrovert, I might have amassed a huge number of friends in different schools in several states. Being an introvert, I gave up on having a friend. Despair found fertile soil. *Things will never change.*

Humans are not very good at peering into the next chapter of life, but God is. Read what He says through the prophet Jeremiah, who lived in such a time of national despair that he is called the weeping prophet. "For I know the thoughts that I think toward you, says the LORD, thoughts of peace and not of evil, to give you a future and a hope" (Jeremiah 29:11).

How important is this hope that God promises? In the 1950s, Dr. Curt Richter performed a series of horrific experiments on Norwegian field rats at the University of California in Berkeley.

Researchers dumped the rats into a tub of water to see how long they could swim before drowning. Results varied, but in general, wild rats died within minutes while domesticated rats swam for days.

Richter reflected that the surprising difference might be a matter of hope. He then repeated the experiment on the wild rats with one exception. When a rat became exhausted, researchers lifted him out of the water and let him recover. Then the experiment was repeated. Instead of mere minutes, the wild rats that had been rescued swam for days before giving up. Curt wrote that *"the rats quickly learn that the situation is not actually hopeless"* and that *"after elimination of hopelessness the rats do not die."*

God paid a tremendous price to light the flame of hope in your heart. You need to tend the fire.

Have there been moments when you've felt as though you couldn't go on? That no one would ever lift you up? Take hope from Jeremiah's words. God has a plan for your life. Had I known at thirteen that within four years I'd be attending a Christian college on a full scholarship, I would have been filled with joy instead of looking for a way to kill myself. No one should give up hope. God paid a tremendous price to light the flame of hope in your heart. He's given you the job of tending the fire.

Some of you may be protesting. *Hey! That's not my life. I'm in the pits, and the last guy to climb out pulled the ladder up after him. There's no way out of this mess.* I suppose the people most entitled to that point of view would be prisoners of war.

I've read the inmates of Nazi concentration camps refrained from waking a comrade having a nightmare, because their reality was worse than any dream. Yet when no one could see a way out, Corrie Ten Boom and her sister Betsy huddled around a smuggled Bible they read to the other women. The flame of hope burned, even there.

Fast forward a few years. Corrie trotted the globe as a renowned international speaker, while Betsy had fallen asleep in her Savior's arms. Fast forward a few more years. Corrie, Betsy, you, and I stand on the crystal sea before the throne of God, crowns on our heads, smiles on our faces, and praise on our lips. That's the expectation of the believer.

In a little while, we're going home to live all eternity with our Papa. I don't know what your view looks like right now, but from where I stand, I see the light of eternity dawning bright and clear. Hold onto your hope. We're almost home.

Day 62: Questions for Reflection

1. How do you feel about God's promise of hope?
2. How has God given you hope?
3. On what do you base your hope?
4. Why does your hope vary from day to day?
5. What causes you despair?
6. How do you cope with negative feelings?
7. What encourages you the most?

AFFIRMATION 62:

God wants me to experience hope.

Day 63: My Defenses

"Then the LORD God called to Adam and
said to him, 'Where are you?'" (Gen. 3:9).

The opening pages of the Bible provide a fascinating glimpse into the way God relates to the barriers His wayward children erect. The story is familiar. The first pair disobeys the only rule God has given them and eats the fruit of the forbidden tree. Smitten with fear, they scramble for a leafy hiding place. I'm sure Adam would have preferred a thick wall, but he has no time to construct one. God is on His way. Crouched among the greenery, the guilty man hears the Voice calling, "Adam, where are you?"

Imagine Adam, cold sweat dripping down his back, as he implores the Earth to swallow him before God discovers his flimsy shelter. Will the Creator reach down and grab him by the neck? His fears are unfounded. God, who already knows where Adam is hiding, chooses to respect his pitiful refuge. Instead of hauling him from his leafy sanctuary, as many an earthly parent would have done, God honors his son's free will.

A person with the habit of reading the first few pages of a book and then skipping to the last chapter would find God using the same approach in Revelation. "Behold, I stand at the door and knock. If anyone hears My voice and opens the door, I will come in to him and dine with him, and he with Me" (Rev. 3:20).

He's outside your door, calling and knocking.

Thousands of years after sin estranged the first man from his Creator, God still calls to His children, longing to reestablish the communion lost when Adam ran to hide. Did you notice where God is? He's *outside* your door, calling and knocking. He's not on a drug bust. He didn't bring the SWAT team. He won't kick your door down. No, the Creator of the universe stands outside your flimsy barriers, knocking and calling you.

The text doesn't tell us *what* God is calling, but I suspect he's calling your name, as He did Adam's. He hopes you'll unbolt the door and invite Him in. The moment you do, it's party time! He eats with you. Maybe He even provides the food, as Jesus did when He cooked breakfast for His disciples by the Sea of Galilee.

What if you don't open the door? Perhaps God weeps, as Jesus did over Jerusalem, but no matter how much your rejection hurts, He won't break in. That's not the way He operates.

Day 63: Questions for Reflection

1. When did you first want to hide?
2. What types of barriers have you built?
3. How well have your defenses worked?
4. Who have you allowed into your refuge?
5. When is God welcome to come in?
6. How often have you heard God knocking?
7. What would it take for you to open the door?

AFFIRMATION 63:

God is knocking at my door.

Day 64:
Dealing with Defenses

"For we do not wrestle against flesh and blood,
but against principalities, against powers, against
the rulers of the darkness of this age, against spiritual hosts of wickedness in the heavenly places"
(Eph. 6:12).

Having come this far, you may be ready to step out of your former lifestyle into freedom. If only a snap of the fingers or a click of the heels would suffice! For years, I assumed ridding myself of harmful defenses would be easy. I'd simply ask God to make short work of my ill-conceived fortress. Life doesn't work that way. God closed His wrecking business. That means *I* have work to do.

Fortunately, I don't have to work alone, and you don't either. Once you open the door, God will keep His part of the bargain to come in and dine with you. That meal will provide the energy to start your demolition, and He's promised to get in the yoke with you and help you haul the rubble away. No magic, just support.

Don't expect God to remove the barriers you've burned into your neural pathways. He sometimes engineers an instantaneous deliverance, but more often He invites His child to partner with Him. God's creation moves in a continual cycle of regeneration—tearing down the old and rebuilding with the new. He invites you to join Him. When invaders reduced the walls of Jerusalem to heaps of rubble, God didn't call in an angelic construction crew. He used human hands to complete the work.

Don't expect God to remove the barriers you've burned into your neural pathways.

No magic wand will erase your past, but you've learned that God's methods, no matter how foolish or inefficient they seem, are always best. If He asks *you* to demolish your walls, you need the exercise. You won't build strong spiritual muscle any other way. In Nehemiah 6:15, you read that the walls of Jerusalem were rebuilt in a mere fifty-two days, less than two months. God empowers you to do amazing things when you ask Him. Here's a sample prayer:

Here I am, Lord. Some of my walls have tumbled already, but others need a push. I throw the door open. Please come in. The place is a mess, but I don't know where to begin. I'm relying on Your promise to complete the work You began in me. Thank You for loving me. Please reveal every barrier I've built and grant me the courage, strength, and perseverance to tear them down in Jesus's name. Amen

Day 64: Questions for Reflection

1. How strong are your walls?
2. What benefits has hiding provided?
3. When will you invite God to come in?
4. What does God want you to do with your past?
5. How much have you been expecting of God?
6. What is God willing to do for you?
7. When are you going to ask for His help?

AFFIRMATION 64:

God won't demolish my defenses.

DAY 65: DEMOLISHING WALLS

"For the weapons of our warfare are not carnal but mighty in God for pulling down strongholds, casting down arguments and every high thing that exalts itself against the knowledge of God, bringing every thought into captivity to the obedience of Christ" (2 Cor. 10:4-5).

Above the scale in my gynecologist's office, a cartoon of an obese woman stepping onto a scale bore the caption: "Hope springs eternal."

On a nearby sticky note, a patient had scrawled, "A taste on the lips stays on the hips."

Ah! Weight is more math than magic.

Consume more calories than you burn, and the excess is deposited as fat. Consume fewer calories than you need, and you burn fat as energy. I've proved it in an animal experiment. A friend, eyeing my Labrador, exclaimed, "Your dog's fat. You're supposed to be able to see her ribs."

I put a little less food in the dog dish each day, and within a month, Cinder was the perfect weight. That was easy.

The mind works the same general way, though removing a mass of harmful beliefs is trickier than shedding a few pounds. Thoughts you indulge repeatedly are deposited in your belief system, eventually snowballing into a mindset that seems truer each time you open the file, *whether or not there is any basis in reality*. Removing faulty thoughts involves bringing the error to light, repeatedly refuting the lie, and overwriting the mistake with truth.

Goebbels, the mastermind of Hitler's Propaganda Bureau, is credited with saying, "If you tell a big enough lie often enough, people will believe it."

Voila! Twisted thinking is the result of psychological warfare; a surreal battle in which you've unwittingly sabotaged yourself! You have either listened to the enemy's lies for so long that you believe them, or you've told yourself a lie that your experiences *seemed* to reinforce.

Removing a mass of harmful beliefs is trickier than shedding a few pounds.

For instance, I may decide I'm ugly because I have a broken tooth. How silly is that? I'll bet you're already thinking of a lie you've told yourself. *I can't sing. I'm clumsy. I never think of the right thing to say.* Or you may decide a coworker despises you because he passes in the hall without a word, when he may simply have a headache.

Once you realize a glob of lies may be burdening your mind, you no longer believe every thought. The world changes from a two-dimensional line drawing into a three-dimensional rainbow. You long to step into that beauty, but a mountain of lies blocks your way. Before you can enter reality, you'll have to deal with your own version of fake news by embracing truth more heartily than you embraced lies.

"Finally, brethren, whatever things are true, whatever things are noble, whatever things are just, whatever things are pure, whatever things are lovely, whatever things are of good report; if there is any virtue, and if there is anything praiseworthy—meditate on these things" (Phil. 4:8).

In other words, you shouldn't entertain every thought that comes knocking. You need to vet them, welcoming the wholesome and dismissing the rotten. Had I followed that protocol, most of my thoughts wouldn't have passed the first criterion, truth. They certainly were neither pure nor lovely. How many of your thoughts pass muster?

As surely as you are what you eat, you are also what you think, or as computer buffs are fond of saying, "Garbage in, garbage out." Let God take out the garbage of enemy lies. Then fill your mind with the truth of God's word, but cut yourself some slack. No one became fat overnight, and no one gets thin in a day. If you've spent years with twisted thinking, you may have to work a little or a lot to get your head on straight. Don't let anything stop you. The rewards are tremendous.

Day 65: Questions for Reflection

1. How easily can you break a habit?
2. Where did you get your belief system?
3. How much of your thinking is accurate?
4. Are more of your ideas beneficial or harmful?
5. What prevents reprogramming your thoughts?
6. How could an accountability partner help?
7. What are the benefits of balanced thinking?

AFFIRMATION 65:

God will teach me to tear down my walls.

Day 66:
Goodbye, Perfection

"He is the Rock, His work is perfect; For all His ways are justice, A God of truth and without injustice; Righteous and upright is He" (Deut. 32:4).

Yes, God is perfect. We are *not* perfect. Neither are the flawed humans we trust. The dentist I contacted about replacing my abscessed front teeth with implants was confident he could help, and the oral surgeon promised no one would even *know* I was having work done. HA! That promise was good until the exciting day when a temporary bridge was installed with *very* temporary glue.

"If that bridge should pop off," the dentist said, "just re-glue it with some of this denture adhesive."

I accepted the tiny tube with a confident smile. I wasn't going to need adhesive. I'd had lots of temporary crowns, and not one had ever come off. DOUBLE HA! Five days later, while brushing my teeth, the gorgeous bridge popped off, leaving me with a ghastly grin of gray tubing. *Okay, don't panic. Just glue it back in. Whoops! I didn't get it pushed up far enough. Now I can't close my mouth. Lord, help me. I'll have to try again. Whew! That's where it goes.*

The next day, the specialist, whose office was two hours away, suggested a local dentist might be willing to re-glue the bridge. Yes, he would—for $130! I'd have to make do with denture adhesive for a *month! That's okay. I can handle this. It may never come off again.* TRIPLE HA!

Three days later, I was giving instructions to my high school Spanish class when my four front teeth slid down. The eyes of the student in front of me widened. I think my heart stopped! Grabbing my straying bridge, I held it in with my thumb while I finished my sentence, then ran to find a quiet place with a mirror. *Whew!* I had survived the unthinkable. The whole world, or at least one student, now knew my front teeth were not real. Could anything worse happen? Yes, it could.

A few days later, the bridge slipped while I was singing on the worship team in front of the church. I managed to hold it up with my lip and tongue for two choruses before I ran for the restroom. Having sixty seconds to return to the stage, I squeezed out so much adhesive that I cemented my upper lip to my gums and couldn't smile for the rest of the service.

What did I learn from these humbling experiences? Much, but nothing about the reliability of dentists or adhesives. By surviving my worst nightmare, I realized I don't have to be perfect! No one is going to reject me if my flaws are showing. By the way, no one even mentioned these incidents. Dropping my front teeth wasn't a big deal to anyone but me.

I wonder what your worst nightmare is; the one you work so hard to hide. If the whole world suddenly knew your most shameful secret, would you survive? You're not sure, are you? If the worst thing you've done were displayed on a billboard today, your fleeting embarrassment might be little more than a funny story tomorrow.

If the whole world suddenly knew your most shameful secret, would you survive?

Day 66: Questions for Reflection

1. In what ways have you striven to be perfect?
2. What would happen if you failed?
3. In which areas are you comfortable being imperfect?
4. When did you first need to be perfect?
5. What happened that created this need?
6. How could you stop striving?
7. Who would you be if you admitted your flaws?

AFFIRMATION 66:

I release the need to be perfect.

Day 67:
Hello, Mistakes

"For we all stumble in many things. If anyone does not stumble in word, he is a perfect man, able to bridle the whole body" (James 3:2).

I watched on television as Michelle Kwan won her fifth ladies' title for the United States at the 2003 World Figure Skating Championships. A whimsical blonde named Elena Sokolova, who hadn't qualified for worlds in five years, took second place for Russia with near-perfect scores. Third place was a tug-of-war between Sasha Cohen of the United States and Fumie Suguri of Japan.

Cohen still had a chance to take the bronze medal when she glided onto the ice for the longer event. Commentators replayed the jumps in slow motion to explain the incorrect angle of a skate at touchdown and how she'd landed on two feet instead of one as she came out of a triple lutz. I wouldn't have noticed those technicalities, but a moment later, Sasha made an error the whole world recognized. She fell down! She jumped up and continued her routine, only to fall again.

I winced when a reporter shoved a microphone in Cohen's face as she left the ice and asked what she thought of her performance. Having just fallen *twice* in front of 16,000 people and millions of television viewers, she smiled and said she was *happy* with her performance. I knew then she was a winner. Champions understand it's okay to make a mistake. Despite two falls and an awkward landing, she beat the Japanese skater in that event, but her competitor had a big enough lead from other rounds to take the bronze medal. Cohen's mistakes may have cost her a medal, but they couldn't destroy her. She had learned to take them in stride.

Some of you are probably thinking: *Wait a minute. It's not okay to make a mistake! Errors can be fatal.* You're right, of course. Because Lori Piestewa, a Hopi servicewoman from Tuba City, Arizona, took a wrong turn in Iraq during the 2003 conflict, her children had to grow up without a mother. But before we generalize, let's ask how many wrong turns are fatal. Most mistakes lead to little more than the loss of a few minutes, and, during those "lost" minutes, the opportunity to explore new territory.

If wrong turns were fatal one percent of the time, many of us would not be alive today. Safety *is* important. Always wear your seat belt, and check your gas gauge periodically. I ran out of gas once on my way to Vacation Bible School with a carload of children. I suppose that *could* have been fatal, but an elderly Hawaiian man took me to a gas station, drove me back to my car, and got me on the road, a pleasant adventure.

Your mistakes probably number in the millions. Most of them have been excellent learning experiences. A presenter at the eighth annual Digital Storytelling Festival in Sedona, Arizona, said our deepest insights come from our most painful experiences. You may wish he were mistaken, but you know the truth when you hear it.

Occasionally, you'll discover your "mistake" was the best thing you could have imagined. You may never have the occasion to mess up in front of 16,000 people, but I hope that if you do, you'll have the courage to smile as genuinely as Sasha Cohen did. Life is too sweet to waste on obsessing over mistakes. It's okay. Really!

Our deepest insights come from our most painful experiences.

Day 67: Questions for Reflection

1. Rate your worst mistake on a scale of one to ten.
2. What happened as a result of this error?
3. How did you benefit from this mishap?
4. How comfortable are you with taking risks?
5. In what ways has avoiding errors hampered you?
6. How do you feel about a mistake you made today?
7. How should children be taught to view their mishaps?

AFFIRMATION 67:

It's okay to make a mistake.

DAY 68:
SICK DAYS

"Is anyone among you sick? Let him call for the elders of the church, and let them pray over him, anointing him with oil in the name of the Lord" (James 5:14).

Were you inculcated with the idea that being sick is bad, almost forbidden? Sickness is an inconvenience, an expense, and a nuisance, but I hope you're free to admit illness because few people make it through life without taking a sick day. For seven years, I worked as the only science substitute at Punahou School, a prestigious private academy in Honolulu, Hawaii. The science department had a dozen teachers, and I often worked two or three days a week, usually in biology or chemistry.

The department chairman, one of two physics teachers, covered for the other. He, himself, was *never* sick. A former Navy SEAL, he taught for over twenty years without taking a day off, a record my husband attempted to match. The result? Hubby once went to school so sick he couldn't speak. *Didn't he care that he was exposing a hundred students to a nasty bug?* He said *they* were the ones who had given him the virus, so they had already *been* exposed. Humans have excellent powers of rationalization. I suspect he thought being sick was not okay.

So, when I took a teaching job at a junior college, I determined never to be absent. I managed perfect attendance for six years.

188

During the seventh year, my madness was arrested by a case of the flu, which left me too weak to get out of bed. As I lay there, reading Thoreau's *Walden,* I reflected on the fact that I wasn't Wonder Woman. My mother might have gone to work so weak she had to hold onto the steam table to keep from falling into the stew, but that didn't mean I had to follow in her footsteps. Flat on my back, I resolved to reform. Not easy!

Admitting you're sick is tantamount to declaring you're human; a frail creature susceptible to any number of maladies. When I returned to high school teaching two years ago, the new principal made it clear he disapproved of teacher absences because substitutes were never as effective. Bingo!

My old programming sprang to life. The district allotted each teacher five days of sick leave and five days of personal leave. I would impress the principal by not using any of them. I made it through the first year fine. The following year, I woke up the day before winter break with laryngitis. Off to school, I went, standing at my classroom door with a sign which read, "You don't want to shake my hand—I'm sick."

"You should have stayed home," the students said. They were right.

In my second year, the stakes were higher. The school board offered a five-hundred-dollar bonus to teachers with perfect attendance. Voila! Instead of one teacher, half the faculty had perfect attendance! Not having budgeted $7,500 for incentives, the school board withdrew the program the following year.

Maybe you, too, should reconsider the idea of going to work sick. Perfect attendance is laudable, but you are a person, not a robot, and people get sick.

Admitting you're sick is tantamount to declaring you're human.

Day 68: Questions for Reflection

1. What was the rule in your house about being sick?
2. How were you treated when you were ill?
3. How do you feel about being indisposed?
4. When did you try to have perfect attendance?
5. How many days do you spend in bed in a year?
6. How do you feel about resting when you're not well?
7. What do you say to yourself when you're sick?

AFFIRMATION 68:

It's okay to get sick.

Day 69:
What You Don't Know

"If any of you lacks wisdom, let him ask of God, who gives to all liberally and without reproach, and it will be given to him" (James 1:5).

As soon as you could babble, "Mama," and "Dada" to your parents' satisfaction, they began to teach you the all-important "magical" words. These mystical phrases were vital to your socialization. Each family has its own list, but high on each parent's agenda are the simple pleasantries: "Please" and "Thank you." You may have balked at begging until you discovered how effective those words proved. "Please give me a cookie" produced better results than "Gimme cookie!"

After you mastered "Please," you were ready for the all-important relationship mender, "I'm sorry." That one was a little harder because ego got in the way, but the results were impressive. I wonder why parents don't include other helpful phrases.

Decades passed before I discovered the magic in the simple words, "I don't know." I suspect my mother never learned that phrase. I can't remember her ever admitting she didn't know something. Until we do, no matter how apparent our bumbling, those about us leave us to struggle on our own. The moment we confess we have no idea what we're doing, help pours in. Why is asking so difficult? Humility is required.

Did your parents seem as all-knowing as mine? When I was a child, I thought my mother knew everything. She knew how to move her family from coast to coast five times without a job on the other end or enough money in her pocket to buy the waitress uniform she would need when she got there. She knew how to paint a house, pluck a chicken, plant a garden, arc weld, and manage a restaurant, but I'm sure there were things Mother *didn't* know. If she was aware of any lack, she was excellent at hiding it.

I wonder about your childhood. Did you think your parents knew everything, and you were magically supposed to know everything, too? Did you feel inadequate when you were expected to perform a task and didn't have the slightest notion how? I did. I didn't inherit the bravado that carried Mother through life with such apparent ease, and I've never been good at hiding my feelings.

Watching me make a cucumber salad one day, Mother gasped as I reached for the mayonnaise. "Don't you know how to make the dressing for cucumber salad?"

"No, I guess I don't," I replied.

She opened the refrigerator. "It's milk with a little vinegar and sugar." She stirred the ingredients into a bowl. "I think you'll like it better."

I did, lots better. It tasted like the cucumber salad I'd enjoyed all my childhood. I'd never have learned to make that dressing if I hadn't said the magic words, "I don't know."

Those words aren't really that difficult to say. Since nobody knows everything, admitting you don't know something is simply stating the obvious. Try it. You'll discover how magical those words can be.

Admitting you don't know something is simply stating the obvious.

Day 69: Questions for Reflection

1. How much did your parents seem to know?
2. Were you expected to know things you'd never been taught?
3. How easily do you admit you don't know something?
4. What happens when you admit your ignorance?
5. When can you safely say, "I don't know?"
6. How do you feel about others admitting they don't know something?
7. What good has come from asking for help?

AFFIRMATION 69:

It's okay to not know everything.

Day 70:
The Anger Problem

"He who is slow to anger is better than the mighty,
And he who rules his spirit than he who takes a city"
(Prov. 16:32).

Is your anger difficult to control? I don't know how your parents handled their anger, but I know their method had a profound effect on you, especially on how comfortable you feel with expressions of emotion. I grew up with an alcoholic father who flew into rages. No one was safe from his wrath. After ten years, my mother left him, but like many battered women, she married another alcoholic, a man who once beat her so severely she lay in bed for three days.

Having spent the first seventeen years of my life in a volatile environment where anyone might be attacked at any moment, I expended a great deal of energy trying to keep everyone happy. By the time I escaped to college, my soul badly scarred, life had become a delicate dance of reading and interpreting the body language of others. I was careful to modify my behavior so no one *ever* got angry. Nobody talked about post-traumatic stress syndrome in those days before Vietnam. I considered my people-pleasing holy. Little did I know my behavior wasn't even Christian!

Many were angry with Christ when He walked the Earth, some of them the most influential men of His day; yet the Savior never modified His behavior to placate them. At His trial, He even refused to answer their questions. Because He was His own man,

He was free to be God's Man, and if I want to be God's woman, people may be enraged with me, too. As Jesus explained, "If you were of the world, the world would love its own. Yet because you are not of the world . . . therefore the world hates you" (John 15:19).

Are you rethinking anger? God's wrath is a frequent theme of scripture. The Bible says He created mankind in His image, which includes a full range of emotions—even anger. Psychologists say this volatile emotion protects the delicate inner life. When hurt, you instinctively feel anger, which empowers you to resolve the problem, relieve the pain, or prevent further abuse.

Anger was *not* the problem in my home. The difficulty lay in the manner in which it was expressed. Did my father's actions stem from bottled-up pain that had been allowed to fester? Instead of confronting their pain, some choose to dull it with a mind-deadening drug, but the anesthetized pain is still smoldering, waiting to flare into rage.

Safety requires an open atmosphere where everyone expresses displeasure and resolves conflicts as they arise. Don't get me wrong, I'm not advocating cutting others to shreds with your tongue. The Bible has a great deal to say about *controlling* the tongue and even more to say about being *slow to anger*, but it *never* suggests repressing emotions.

On the contrary, the apostle Paul admonishes: "Be angry, and do not sin: do not let the sun go down on your wrath" (Ephesians 4:26).

You can expect others to get angry with you. That's life. Imperfect as you are, you *will* forget a promise, or fail in a duty, or rub someone the wrong way. You can even expect to get riled *yourself*. Being upset is part of being human, and it's okay. Really.

You can expect others to get angry with you. That's life.

Day 70: Questions for Reflection

1. How did your parents express anger?
2. How did you feel about their method?
3. What have you suffered from others' ill will?
4. How were you allowed to express anger?
5. Are you usually aware of your disgust?
6. How do you express displeasure today?
7. How has anger helped you make decisions?

AFFIRMATION 70:

It's okay if someone gets angry with me.

Day 71:
Feeling Unloved

"The LORD has appeared of old to me, saying: 'Yes, I have loved you with an everlasting love; Therefore with lovingkindness I have drawn you'" (Jer. 31:3).

Have you ever felt like an outcast, the ugly duckling, the clumsy oaf no one wanted on their team? Am I the only one who's had difficulty feeling as though I were part of a group? You probably haven't heard, "I don't like you," or worse, "I hate you," since elementary school, when friendships were forged and broken as quickly as ice cream melts on a summer sidewalk.

Adults don't usually revert to such childishness. They avert their eyes, turn their heads, or stare at their phones while you're attempting to engage with them. The result is the same as the harsh words flung around at kindergarten recess. You feel like an outsider, and being an outsider hurts.

Humans are adept at forming groups. People gather in churches, bars, baseball clubs, motorcycle gangs, and volunteer associations, to name a few. No one voices the unwritten rule: stray too far from group dogma and you're out. Everyone knows you either agree with the group's stand or you find yourself an outsider, wondering if there's any place you fit.

Teaching at Sedona Red Rock High School, I considered myself an outsider. In faculty meetings, vocal teachers appeared to be of the opposite political persuasion, mourning election results that delighted me. One woman declared yoga to be her religion. Were there Christians in the group? In brainstorming sessions where my suggestions were sometimes ignored, I stopped making them. Having only thirty minutes for lunch, I didn't eat with anyone, nor was I invited to join the half-dozen who gathered across the hall for lunch. I was pretty much a loner.

You can't really be anyone except the person God created you to be.

Imagine my surprise when a group of ladies rallied around me with cards and flowers when they learned I would be having surgery the next week. I had to admit I'd been wrong. I did have friends on the faculty. How quickly we jump to conclusions, amassing evidence that agrees with our original premise and ignoring the rest. I'd been wrong for ten years! I had always been an insider, despite feeling excluded.

Although being part of a group is vital to your growth, being accepted is not the most important aspect of life. I challenge you to stand up for what you believe, even if you have to stand alone. Being true to yourself is important, and the moment you take the risk of voicing your opinion, you'll cheer. *Yes! For the first time in my life, I stood up for myself!* You'll be miserable until you do. Besides, you may be surprised to discover others who agree with you.

Most people won't say, "I don't like you" to your face, but they may wander off, leaving you alone. That's okay. You can't really be anyone except the person God created you to be, so, above all, be true to yourself. Remember, you're already a member of the most important group, God's family.

Day 71: Questions for Reflection

1. How well were you accepted as a child?
2. What is your identity: likes and dislikes?
3. When did you sacrifice your identity for approval?
4. How important is being true to yourself?
5. What are you willing to give up to fit in?
6. What happened when someone didn't like you?
7. Who would you prefer *didn't* like you? Why?

AFFIRMATION 71:

It's okay if someone dislikes me.

Day 72:
Not Measuring Up

"But God has chosen the foolish things of the world to put to shame the wise, and God has chosen the weak things of the world to put to shame the things which are mighty; and the base things of the world and the things that are despised God has chosen, and the things which are not, to bring to nothing the things that are" (1 Cor. 1:27-28).

How do you feel when someone *significant* complains that you haven't measured up to their expectations? "I thought you were smarter, cuter, handier, taller, more musical, . . ."

The list is endless. Upon receiving such signals, do you beat yourself up? *What's the matter with me that I'm not smarter, cuter, handier, taller, more musical, or...?*

Feeling deficient, you wonder whether you were born lacking this all-important quality or just failed to develop it. Such thinking does nothing to acquire the missing attribute and probably detracts from the splendid abilities you do possess.

Failing to measure up to someone else's standard can be a minor affair. Imagine standing at the counter of your local fast-food restaurant with a friend. After you've ordered a triple cheeseburger, your pal looks at you in amazement and exclaims, "I thought you were a vegetarian!"

Not many people will ditch a buddy for laying his teeth into a chunk of fried flesh, so you're probably safe to laugh and order extra mustard.

However, there are other times when failing to meet expectations carries grave consequences. When your employer says the company is laying off everyone who doesn't have a master's degree, and you're first on the list, that's serious. If your mate informs you that you're unsuitable and the marriage is over, you're facing a significant loss. How are you supposed to respond to your inability to measure up in those circumstances?

A. Cry
B. Go back to school for more training
C. Swear
D. Look for another job or another mate
E. All of the above
F. None of the above

When faced with one of these weightier scenarios, I try to remember that people are different. God made us that way so we would complement one another in a delicate dance of interdependence. Our differing personalities, talents, and aptitudes guarantee none of us is good at everything; each of us is good at something, and most of us are good at a great many things. When someone implies they are disappointed with me, I say to myself, *Poor fellow, he's too distracted by his expectations to appreciate the amazing qualities I do have!*

You *are* marvelous, whether or not you are vivacious, have a working knowledge of Microsoft Word, or can complete a marathon in less than five hours. If you *want* to run a marathon, more power to you. But if you, like me, have never felt the urge to put your body through an ordeal of that magnitude, you don't *need* to prove anything to anyone.

God has uniquely gifted you, and He's still bringing those gifts to maturity.

Although Jesus was perfect, He was criticized at every turn, yet He was so focused on pleasing His Father that neither the praise nor the criticism of men affected Him. You can begin to adopt His attitude. When someone implies you've failed, remind yourself that God has uniquely gifted you, and He's still bringing those gifts to maturity. In the meantime, smile at those who voice their disapproval and remember that you're God's masterpiece.

Day 72: Questions for Reflection

1. When were you told you didn't measure up?
2. How did you process your feelings?
3. Were the expectations reasonable?
4. How do your failings affect you?
5. How important is pleasing others?
6. How does God regard your failings?
7. What progress has God made in you?

AFFIRMATION 72:

It's okay if I don't measure up.

Day 73:
Expressing Emotions

"Open rebuke is better than love
carefully concealed" (Prov. 27:5).

I know expressing emotions is okay because well-known biblical prophets did just that. Almost everyone remembers the story of Jonah and the big fish. According to the short book which bears his name, Jonah, when asked to deliver a message of doom to Nineveh, promptly booked passage on a ship headed in the opposite direction. Asleep in the hold when a horrendous storm threatened the vessel, Jonah was awakened by a sailor urging him to call on his God.

Every man aboard was desperately imploring whatever god he served to save their lives. At last, the men thought to cast lots to determine the cause of their calamity. Ah ha! When the lot fell on Jonah, he confessed his disobedience to the Creator God and instructed the men to toss him overboard to save their skins. Horrified, the sailors tried everything else to no avail. Then down into the murky depths they flung the sorry prophet. The storm calmed instantly, and the Lord, who wasn't finished with Jonah, sent a great fish to swallow His disobedient son.

In the belly of the fish for three wet, stinky days, Jonah repented of his rebellion, so God told the fish to vomit him out on dry land. The beast, more obedient than the man, promptly did as God commanded. Jonah then wiped the seaweed out of his hair and walked into the great heathen city, crying, "Forty days and Nineveh will be destroyed."

Imagine the hysteria! Everyone, including the king, repented in sackcloth and ashes! Even the animals participated in fasting and wearing sackcloth. Can you hear the heart-wrenching wails rising to heaven? If Noah's preaching had brought that response, he wouldn't have needed an ark.

Was the runaway prophet turned inner-city evangelist ecstatic at his success? Quite the contrary! When God accepted the Ninevites' repentance and rescinded their death sentence, Jonah was disgusted. How dare God change His mind! Let's listen to his complaint.

"'Ah, LORD, was not this what I said when I was still in my country? Therefore I fled previously to Tarshish; for I know that You are a gracious and merciful God, ... Therefore now, O LORD, please take my life from me, for it is better for me to die than to live!'"

Then the LORD said, "'Is it right for you to be angry'" (Jonah 4:2-4).

God gave Jonah an opportunity to discuss his hurt feelings, but like a sullen child, the seer didn't answer. He retreated to a hillside outside the city to watch and wait. When the sun became too hot, he built a little booth to shade his head. Then God made a vine spring up to protect the perspiring prophet. The next day, while Jonah was enjoying the relief, God sent a worm to eat the vine and a wind to blow the withered remnants away. About to faint, Jonah exploded.

"'It is better for me to die than to live.' Then God said to Jonah, 'Is it right for you to be angry about the plant?' And he said, 'It is right for me to be angry, even to death'" (Jonah 4: 8-9)!

This time, God didn't drop the subject. He suggested that if the prophet cared so much about a vine that grew up and died in a day, the God of the universe should care about a city in which there were more than 120,000 people who didn't know their right hand from their left.

God won't be satisfied until you tell Him what's wrong, so don't hold back.

Not many have merited a conversation with God. Jonah did, because God considered the seer's upset feelings reason to call a conference. God didn't say, "Grow up!" He didn't say, "Stuff it." He reasoned with His angry child. The book closes without telling us whether Jonah got over his tantrum.

Are you, like Jonah, able to tell God what's bothering you, or do you pretend you're not angry? God won't be satisfied until you tell Him what's wrong, so don't hold back. He already knows what you're feeling.

Day 73: Questions for Reflection

1. Which feelings were taboo in your home?
2. As a child, were you allowed to express anger?"
3. Which feelings are more comfortable?
4. How do you feel when others express emotions you avoid?
5. Which feelings qualify for your no-no list? Why?
6. How do you avoid feelings you've blacklisted?
7. How should you deal with "negative" emotions?

AFFIRMATION 73:

It's okay to feel, even to feel angry.

Day 74: Angry with God?

"So the LORD said to Cain, 'Why are you angry? And why has your countenance fallen? If you do well, will you not be accepted? And if you do not do well, sin lies at the door. And its desire is for you, but you should rule over it" (Gen. 4:6-7).

I was praying as I drove the coast highway from Hawaii Kai to Waimanalo. Rounding a curve, I glimpsed the spectacular stretch of ocean that reaches from Rabbit Island to Molokai. As I soaked in the beauty of foaming waves, I heard God asking me to surrender my past to Him, to nail the whole slimy glob to the cross and get on with my life.

As the gorgeous seascape glided past my windshield, I began to cry so hard I could barely see the low stone wall separating my narrow lane from a hundred-foot drop-off. "Are you saying everything that happened to me was *okay*?" I yelled. "That was *not* okay! Do you hear me? THAT WAS NOT OKAY!" No reply.

Undone, I turned into the parking lot of a church and let my angry tears flow. God didn't zap me. He held me in His arms until I stopped sobbing, but my tantrum didn't convince Him to withdraw His request. No responsible parent changes their mind because their youngster cries. God knew my anger was born of the pain I insisted on clutching to my breast; pain He wanted me to release. There in the church yard, under the fragrant branches of a white plumeria tree, I saw God was right, and I gave Him my past, the whole yucky blob.

I tend to cry or shout when I'm angry. You may be more prone to swear. Is it okay to swear at God? We walk a narrow line when we speak of cursing the God who is so glorious no man can gaze upon His face and live. He is the holy One to be revered, obeyed, and loved above all else, but He is also our Father. How does a father handle temper tantrums? He adapts his tactics to the maturity of the child.

A friend of mine began to seek the Lord in earnest when his ten-year marriage disintegrated. Being a serviceman, he had doubt-less heard every unsavory word, although I never heard him utter one. In his despair, he took to the jogging track, and as he ran, he cursed—God! When he had exhausted his supply of curse words, only the slap of his feet on the track punctuated the silence. Then God said, "My precious son." After all that?

God realizes you're upset before you do. Acknowledging your emotions is the first step to a deeper relationship, both with Him and with others. You don't expect to grow close to another human being without becoming upset with them. Why should you expect to get close to God without feeling angry? *Why doesn't my all-pow-erful Friend do what I'm sure He should?*

Your ire may be misguided, but it's real. The God who made you knows your understanding is limited. Run to Him with your hurts, and He'll deal with them as only a loving Father can.

Acknowledging your emotions is the first step to deeper relationships with God and others.

Day 74: Questions for Reflection

1. How did you handle your childhood anger?
2. How did your parents react?
3. Which expressions of anger caused discomfort?
4. When were you upset with God?
5. What did you do with those feelings?
6. How can you be respectful and angry at the same time?
7. What does God want you to do with your anger?

AFFIRMATION 74:

It's okay to be angry with God.

Day 75:
Releasing Anger

"Love suffers long and is kind; love does not envy; love does not parade itself, is not puffed up; does not behave rudely, does not seek its own, is not provoked, thinks no evil" (1 Cor. 13:4-5).

Hot-air balloons often float over the red rocks of Sedona, Arizona, in the early morning. The colorful globes, powered by burners producing a roar audible on the ground, lift several people high into the air. The principle is simple: the skin of the balloon traps the heated air, which is less dense than the atmosphere and, therefore, lighter. Up, up, and away! The balloon ascends on the gentle breeze.

Because Arizona is hot in the summer, tourists sometimes have to rise as early as 3:00 a.m. to enjoy a balloon ride. Once the summer sun is well up, the operators deflate their airships and cart them away. I've seen the basket-like gondolas going down the road, but not the majestic envelopes, which have been folded into insignificant heaps.

For years, I operated like a hot-air balloon, soaring high above the landscape, puffed up and given shape by a roaring burner of anger I wasn't conscious of harboring. Anger's insidious flame made me feel powerful enough to rise above life. I could soar! I was majestic! I was also alone, but that didn't seem to matter as much as escaping. Every balloon comes down eventually. The question is where. A gouge in the asphalt in front of my house bears mute testimony to the fact that they don't always land where the operator would prefer. Neither did I.

Once I realized I was running on anger and the resulting adrenaline, I wanted to plant my feet firmly on the ground where I could smell the honeysuckle, but my desire was tempered by fear. I had been running my burner on high for so many years that my anger had morphed into bitterness, resentment, and rage. This unholy trinity had been holding me hostage for a long time. So long that I was afraid. Would there be anything left if I turned off the burner? The keeper of the flame screamed, "NO!"

If you've heard that voice, don't believe him. He's a liar.

Today's scripture says, "love does not parade itself, is not puffed up" (1 Cor. 13:4). Devoid of the love which makes life worth living, I had been puffing myself up to anesthetize the pain. If you've made the same mistake, I have news for you. You can change course. Turn off the burner and release your anger. Then anchor yourself firmly to the ground.

Once you are safely down, you'll discover you still have a shape, though your form may not be clearly defined. Ask God to mold you into a loving contour. It's okay to be in process, and you'll enjoy life much more when you're no longer running on adrenaline. Because you don't need to be perfect, there's no reason to be angry when you're not. Take a deep breath and let out all your hot air. Then relax and get firmly grounded. Fold up that pretentious envelope and stow the gondola. You won't be needing them anymore.

Turn off the burner and release your anger. Then anchor yourself firmly to the ground.

Day 75: Questions for Reflection

1. How did you cope with a hopeless situation?
2. How do you release your anger?
3. When has ire festered into rage or bitterness?
4. How do harbored resentments affect you?
5. How often do you feel a need to defend yourself?
6. What are the benefits and pitfalls of stockpiled anger?
7. What will you do with your stockpile?

AFFIRMATION 75:

It's okay to release my anger.

Day 76:
A Ray of Hope

"Hope deferred makes the heart sick, but when the desire comes, it is a tree of life" (Prov. 13:12).

King Solomon, the wisest and richest man of his generation, penned those sad words. The king had experience in hoping for something he couldn't attain. Perhaps there were things even the richest man couldn't buy; things for which he, like the rest of us, could only hope. In Solomon's case, one of these may have been love, for if I read the "Song of Solomon" correctly, King Solomon had amassed a bevy of women before he found the love of his life. "There are sixty queens, and eighty concubines, and virgins without number. My dove, my perfect one, is the only one" (Song of Solomon 6:8-9).

I knew as a child that life is full of disappointments. Did you? The things you couldn't control left no guarantee you'd receive *anything* for which you hoped. Did you take disappointment well? Or did you decide to expect the worst? Refusing to hope usually brings what you expect. Job noted: "For the thing I greatly feared has come upon me, And what I dreaded has happened to me" (Job 3:25).

Life has an amazing way of fulfilling your fantasies, even the self-destructive ones! Did you realize your refusal to hope was distinctly un-Christian? How can those who serve "the God of all hope" (Rom. 15:13) be hopeless? The easy way out is the coward's way. You can be glad Solomon finishes today's proverb on an optimistic note. "But when the desire comes, it is a tree of life" *(Prov. 13:12).*

A tree of life? In the first pages of the Bible, you read that God planted a tree in the Garden of Eden bearing fruit that could sustain life. When Adam sinned, God stationed cherubim with a flaming sword to bar access to that tree. But He promised in the last pages of the Bible that His children would see the tree of life again, growing on both sides of the river of life in the New Jerusalem. You live in the unhappy middle, between the tree of life removed and the tree of life restored. Where does that leave you?

God has provided a tree of life for those who inhabit this no-man's land between the two Paradises. If you hope in God, you're disappointment-proof, even when you fail to receive the things you hope for! Scripture tells us Abraham, who lived in a tent in the land God had promised him, died without ever finding the city he was seeking! "These all died in faith, not having received the promises, but having seen them afar off were assured of them, embraced them and confessed that they were strangers and pilgrims on the earth" (Hebrews 11:13).

If you hope in God, you win every time—even when you *seem* to have lost. This short, earthly life is only the preamble to eternity. Abraham is going to have his city because he hoped in God's promise. He didn't try to protect himself from disappointment by carping, "Aw, I knew all along there wasn't anything out there but desert."

No. Abraham hugged God's word to his heart and lived every day in eager expectation of the good he was about to receive. He *dared* to hope, and I challenge you to hope with him. Go ahead. Take the dare.

Abraham hugged God's word to his heart and lived every day in eager expectation.

Day 76: Questions for Reflection

1. What did you desperately hope for as a child?
2. When are you hopeful, and when are you cynical?
3. Which would you prefer to be, as a general rule?
4. What would change if you allowed more hope?
5. What promises has God made to *you*?
6. What does God want you to hope for?
7. What secret hope have you never shared?

AFFIRMATION 76:

It's okay to hope.

Day 77:
Never Too Late

"And do not be conformed to this world, but be transformed by the renewing of your mind, that you may prove what is that good and acceptable and perfect will of God" (Rom. 12:2).

Delightfully spry and sharp as a cactus thorn, Lydia Newton was a joy to visit. As we sat in the double rocker in her Sedona, Arizona, home, her bubbly laughter set me giggling, and I sometimes forgot she was almost twice my age. Her days on Earth spanned three centuries, and when she was 111, magazines and newspapers were anxious to know the secret of her longevity. Little did they know Grandma Newton had one bad habit. No, not smoking or drinking. Lydia's bad habit was *not* drinking. She refused to drink water, despite living in Arizona.

"I don't like the taste of it," she shrugged. "As a girl, I loved fresh-churned buttermilk."

Because fresh-churned buttermilk was no longer available, Lydia chose to abstain from drinking completely. Aside from an occasional glass of fruit juice, she drank nothing, and nothing I said could persuade her otherwise. She had been set in her ways for more than a century!

I'm not criticizing my elders. I'm learning from them. I discovered I, too, am set in *my* ways, preferring my comfortable rut to the adventure of blazing a new trail. Can you identify with me? Life gets comfortable, and you want to rest. *Haven't I grown enough? Haven't I learned enough? Haven't I earned the right to relax and enjoy how far I've come?* Not really.

Living things are either growing or decaying, and you'd rather be growing, which involves change. If a rut is a grave with the ends kicked out, you shouldn't stop with kicking out the ends. Spring out and climb to higher ground! You are *not* too old to learn. Even Lydia could have found a drink she enjoyed.

I was fifty years old when I found an undiscovered half of my vocal range above the break I'd always feared to cross. Having sung tenor for decades, I was suddenly soaring into melody. I learned to sing all over again. How exciting! After I had recorded three CDs of my own compositions, I decided to face another fear. In a Yavapai College drawing class, I progressed from stick figures to still lifes to portraits. The most exciting change was still ahead.

After thirty years of teaching Spanish by the grammar method, I attended a workshop touting a new technique. Accustomed to meeting students a year after they had left my class to discover they'd forgotten everything, I instantly adopted Total Physical Response Storytelling (TPRS). My students now reported *remembering* everything. Two boys even returned to tell me they had been tested three years after graduation and received five semesters of college credit in Spanish for their two semesters in high school. Wow!

Bring on the challenges. New frontiers beckon. Don't listen to discouraging voices. You are never too old to learn. "You have turned for me my mourning into dancing; You have put off my sackcloth and clothed me with gladness" (Ps. 30:11). Sadness gives way to celebration when God's in the picture. Is this your day for an upgrade?

New frontiers beckon continually. You're never too old to learn.

Day 77: Questions for Reflection

1. When did you make your first significant change?
2. When did you make your last significant change?
3. How do you feel about change?
4. When have you thought someone was too old to change?
5. What stands between you and the changes you want to effect?
6. Is there ever a time when it's too late to change?
7. What is the biggest impediment to the changes you want to make?

AFFIRMATION 77:

It's never too late to change.

Day 78:
Rigid Thinking

"So he said to Him, 'O my Lord, how can I save Israel? Indeed, my clan is the weakest in Manasseh, and I am the least in my Father's house.' And the LORD said to him, 'Surely I will be with you, and you shall defeat the Midianites as one man'" (Judges 6:15-16).

You might think God would get tired of the excuses His champions give Him, but He knows changing a deeply ingrained mindset is a formidable challenge. Do you believe, as they did, that someone else is more qualified to do the job God has asked of you? Maybe you think you need to break a habit first.

After smoking for forty-five years, my mother attended a Five-Day Plan to Stop Smoking and quit for a month. Over the next five years, she attended two more clinics and stopped each time. But each time, after a month estranged from her old friend Nicotine, she would encounter a stress that *demanded* a cigarette. They calmed her. She promised to smoke *only* one, but one always led to another.

I attended those three valiant efforts with her as she waged a war on two fronts: the physical craving and the psychological attachment. She felt as though she were losing her best friend. I didn't give her enough credit. Each day without a cigarette was a major accomplishment.

Since I've decided to overcome *my* addiction to viewing *everything* as perfectly good or completely evil, I realize how deeply cemented my thought patterns have become. Last week, the leader of the worship team said someone was flat. I winced, probably me. Someone was slow on the pickup. Me again.

In my thinking, I've always been special. I wrestle with well-disguised pride. Being the one who can't do *anything* right gives me status. If there's a problem, *I'm* the cause. I've felt guilty about traffic accidents on the East Coast and floods in China. I'm not sure when I became responsible for the decisions of others and even God, but I *am* sure when I want to stop. Now!

Doomsayers remind you that habits take time to break. Three weeks is often quoted as the magic number. Consider that *good* news because you can do almost anything for three weeks. Besides, God sometimes shortens the time. After my pastor threw his cigarettes out the car window, confessed he *liked* to smoke, and asked God to help him stop, he never felt another urge.

When my son, the thumb-sucker, chewed a nasty sore with his newly-erupted teeth, I put a sock on his hand and pinned it to his shirt as I put him to bed. A week later, I forgot the sock. He never put his thumb in his mouth again. Miracles happen every day. Some qualify for them. Others have to do the hard work, so expect to work hard. God is waiting to boost you out of your self-destructive rut, but you have to ask Him first.

God is waiting to boost you out of your self-destructive rut, but you have to ask Him.

Day 78: Questions for Reflection

1. How have you overcome a deeply ingrained habit?
2. When have you judged others' struggles with habits?
3. How long have you indulged in all-or-none thinking?
4. Has absolute thinking caused you recent pain?
5. How do you plan to reform your thinking?
6. What are your chances of success?
7. Have you asked God to help you think more clearly?

AFFIRMATION 78:

I detect self-defeating thoughts.

DAY 79: READY. SET. GO!

"The soul of a lazy man desires, and has nothing;
But the soul of the diligent shall be made rich"
(Prov. 13:4).

Do you love procrastination as much as I do? I find it positively delicious. I guess I love leaving chores undone *almost* as much as I hate doing them. An old farmer declined an invitation to hear a government specialist because, in his words, "I *already* know more than I'm doing."

He realized something I've been slow to grasp: Knowledge has no value until it's put into practice. Most of us *know* more than we *do*, some of us much more.

In my case, I've known for years that absolute thinking was causing me pain. Yet I persisted, having become strangely accustomed to discomfort. Besides, I had been apprehensive about the prospect of change. You know that queasy feeling that comes when you wonder if the change you're contemplating will prove to be worse than the status quo? Well, no more. This is it. Today's the day for my new start. I'm ready for change. Really!

Since a new start can't be official without a declaration, and a declaration isn't really official until someone else knows about it, I'm writing down my intent, and I'm telling you about it. I suggest you write yours down too. Then sign the paper, date it, and give it to a herald to announce in the town square of your life.

DECLARATION OF INTENT

Hear ye! Hear ye! The following person, _________________, has sworn on the _______ day of _______________ in the year of our Lord _______________, to stop indulging in the harmful and self-destructive habit of absolute thinking. From this day forward, _______________________ vows to distinguish the limited number of true absolutes from their multitudinous impostors. _______________ also determines to distinguish which situations are absolute and which are not, and choose accordingly.

Signed _______________________________

Dated _______________________

Witnessed ___________________________

Having made up your mind, you are ready to assemble your support staff. Believe me, you are going to need one. Drivers don't win the Indianapolis 500 without an excellent pit crew. Pilots bailing out of burning planes wouldn't have a prayer without the dedicated help of those who packed their parachutes. Even the Lone Ranger had Tonto, so don't try to go it alone. Those lost in perfectionism are blind to reality. You need another pair of eyes, but choose carefully. You want a sympathetic, non-condemning cheerleader. If your mate doesn't qualify, select a different accountability partner.

Jesus commented on the uselessness of going off halfcocked. "Or what king, going to make war against another king, does not sit down first and consider whether he is able with ten thousand to meet him who comes against him with twenty thousand? Or else, while the other is still a great way off, he sends a delegation and asks the conditions of peace" (Luke 14:31-32).

Be wise enough to count the cost. You are, after all, declaring war on your shame-based, guilt-ridden mindset. Changing old habits *is* difficult, and absolute thinking is harder to remove than a glob of bubble gum on the sole of your shoe. You can expect your inner dictator to fight back with every weapon in her arsenal, especially the overwhelming sense of false guilt and condemnation that has been so effective in controlling you.

Absolute thinking is harder to remove than a bubble gum on the sole of your shoe.

The days ahead may not be pleasant. War never is. So take stock of your allegiance. Are you ready to fight to the death? This question is not rhetorical. You *may* face days when the battle seems to threaten your very existence. If you persevere, a glorious victory awaits.

What is your freedom worth? Are you ready to join Patrick Henry in his declaration, "Give me liberty, or give me death?"

If you're not, that's okay. Admit it. Then decide if and when you would *like* to be ready, and tell someone the date.

Day 79: Questions for Reflection

1. What disadvantages has procrastination brought?
2. What advantages has procrastination provided?
3. Why delay your shift away from all-or-none thinking?
4. When will you begin to think more rationally?
5. Who would be the best person(s) for your support team?
6. To whom will you read your Declaration of Intent?
7. When will you be ready to say, "Give me liberty or give me death?"

AFFIRMATION 79:

My absolute thinking is deeply ingrained.

DAY 80:
THE PROCESS OF CHANGE

"Therefore we do not lose heart. Even though our outward man is perishing, yet the inward man is being renewed day by day" (2 Cor. 4:16).

On the first day, when students walk into my Spanish classroom, I ask them to formulate their goals for the eighteen-week course. Ninety percent of them want to be fluent in the language. I assume, having undertaken the challenge of attaining fluency in four and a half months, they are prepared to utilize every precious moment of class time for language acquisition. Wrong! They want to watch movies, play games, and talk to their friends (in English, of course), while magically acquiring Spanish. They would be delighted with a magic potion bequeathing instant mastery of the language.

I'm not putting my students down, or, as they would say, dissing them. They are logical products of the age in which we live. The motto of our day seems to be "The faster the better." From microwaves to fast food to direct internet connections, we crave speed. Driving into Phoenix, I spotted a billboard that read, "Hastings and Hastings, Accident Lawyers. It's all about time."

We not only want fast cars, but we also want fast lawyers when we crash them! Banks now advertise next-day loans, a drastic improvement over the three-and-a-half weeks required for approval in 1970. Magazines are filled with articles touting three easy steps to accomplish weight loss, develop more satisfying relationships, and achieve other seemingly complex objectives.

Down deep, you realize most things cannot be achieved quickly and easily, but you prefer to pretend they can. "This doesn't work for me," scowled the first editor to review this book. "You need seven *easy* steps."

I have reservations about the "seven-easy-steps" approach. I fear the reader may become disheartened to find the issue only partially resolved when the cure was purported to be fast and easy. What a shame to abandon the very thing that was working, albeit slowly. Perseverance would have yielded big rewards because change takes time.

A dog trainer once told me the Doberman Pinschers she worked with were uncannily intelligent. One pup could follow a trail without putting its nose to the ground by looking at the flags she'd placed in the trees for humans. If she made one mistake teaching a command, she'd have to spend over twenty hours reprogramming the dog to eradicate the error fully.

Like your furry friends, you don't change easily. The perfectionism you've ingrained will require patience to undo. That process begins with breaking the habit of absolute thinking. As you work to transform your thought patterns, give yourself a break. Old beliefs don't give up easily, so hang in there. Remember, you're an overcomer.

Old beliefs don't give up easily, so hang in there.

Day 80: Questions for Reflection

---

1. What do you like about the fast-and-easy culture?
2. Why do you think speed and effortlessness are supreme?
3. Which deeply ingrained habit have you overcome?
4. How did you make this transformation?
5. How many major transformations have you accomplished?
6. Which aspect of your perfectionism are you ready to reform?
7. What advice would you offer yourself today?

AFFIRMATION 80:

Change takes time and effort.

Day 81:
Energy, Perseverance,
and Wisdom

"You are snared by the words of your mouth; You are taken by the words of your mouth" (Prov. 6:2).

"In the multitude of words sin is not lacking, but he who restrains his lips is wise" (Prov. 10:19).

Do you secretly enjoy those silly Energizer Bunny ads? Watching the little guy keep going despite formidable obstacles, do you cheer inwardly? You want him to beat his drum forever, and he probably could—if someone changed his battery once in a while.

Those ads inspire you because you'd like to be more like that indomitable rabbit. Are you prone to running down, perhaps because you face problems his pink, fuzzy head never encounters? Humans are subject to discouragement, perplexity, and fatigue, which machines don't battle, and when you are run down, you're depleted both mentally and physically.

Have you noticed how much of your fatigue arises from negative self-talk? Every time I took a wrong turn in the road of life, I'd berate my stupidity. Old Pink Ears doesn't beat himself up. He just keeps walking, one tiny step after another, until his perseverance takes him where he's going. There's a lot to be said for perseverance. That's why I decided a few days back to write out my Declaration of Intent and have it read in the village square of my life.

God has promised you certain victory. Don't quibble about which road leads you there.

That declaration serves several purposes. First, you can read it to yourself. Despite your best efforts to be positive, there are times when your internal chatter disintegrates into put-downs. *You'll never succeed. You're too dumb. Why try?* Those inner words do as much harm as the ones you speak out loud.

I suggest you smile slyly, break out your Declaration of Intent, and read it boldly out loud. *Wow! What a wonderful person!* Reading your declaration recharges your battery by reminding you where you've been, who you are, and where you're going. Sure, you *make* mistakes, but you are *not* a mistake. You're a child of God, and He has promised you certain victory. Don't quibble about which road leads you there.

The second purpose of reading your Declaration of Intent aloud is to inform those around you of the proposed changes in your lifestyle. Whether they applaud or groan, you can use their reactions to keep you on task. Soak up the applause and search your heart for traces of the characteristics your enemies attack.

While Israel's King David was fleeing his usurping son Absalom, an evil man named Shimei strode along beside him, hurling dirt and *curses*. David's soldiers wanted to kill Shimei for his insubordination, but David ordered, "Let him alone, and let him curse; for so the LORD has ordered him" (2 Sam. 16:11). Hmmm. Do you have a Shimei? Mine said, "You walk like a man. You blow your nose too loudly. You talk like someone from the hills."

The third purpose of reading your Declaration of Intent aloud is the potential to recruit accountability partners who can remind you of your direction, preventing you from becoming disoriented, discouraged, or overwhelmed. People count, and those God has placed within your sphere of influence come bearing gifts. Sort through the pile, discard the rubbish, and treasure the gems. Who knows? Shimei may be a blessing in disguise. Do I really walk like a man?

Day 81: Questions for Reflection

1. How positive is your self-talk on any given day?
2. How do you react when you make a mistake?
3. What happens to your energy when you put yourself down?
4. When have you used your Declaration of Intent?
5. How do you react when others make a mistake?
6. How high is your energy level today?
7. What could you do to improve your vigor?

AFFIRMATION 81:

I need energy, perseverance, and wisdom.

Day 82:
God Provides

"He gives power to the weak, And to those who have no might, He increases strength . . . . But those who wait on the LORD shall renew their strength; They shall mount up with wings like eagles, they shall run and not be weary, they shall walk and not faint" (Isa. 40:29,31).

Once we've agreed on how valuable self-affirmation is, we need to acknowledge the limitations. Although you accomplish more when you're praising your efforts than when you're berating yourself, cheerleading isn't the panacea it's thought to be. You *can* pull yourself up by your bootstraps, but only so far. Then you need to look up. God not only possesses *infinite* wisdom and power, but He also wants to share them with you.

The entire book of Proverbs is a small portion of His efforts to instruct you in the fine art of knowing what to do in any situation. As for energy, He has promised those who wait upon him will renew their strength, even more than the Energizer Bunny! According to Isaiah 40:31, they not only walk without fainting, but they also fly! Wouldn't you rather soar over your difficulties than crawl along in the dust of your own efforts? Ask God to energize you.

If you prize your independence, you may want to skip this part, particularly if you feel humiliated at the thought of asking for help.

I understand your reticence, but I don't suggest anyone struggle through life alone. You may not get far. Jesus Christ, a full-fledged member of the Godhead, sometimes spent the *entire* night communing with His Father. Why feel bad about *your* need to pray?

I'm not suggesting you pray for an entire night. God is eager to help. He seizes the smallest opportunity to open the windows of heaven and pour a blessing on His children. Your struggle to climb out of the pits of perfectionism is such a moment. Whether you pray for a minute, an hour, or a night, you will receive His power and His assurance. You are not alone. He is with you, pointing the way, urging you on, and even pulling you out of quicksand. "Even to your old age, I am He, And even to gray hairs I will carry you! I have made, and I will bear; even I will carry, and will deliver you" (Isa. 46:4).

When my mother lay dying in a coma 2,000 miles away in California, I was beside myself. Trying to reach her was senseless. Remaining in Hawaii seemed unbearable. I asked my heavenly Father to scoop her up in His strong arms and carry her over the threshold into eternity. I know He did, because He picked me up, too. When I felt those powerful arms around me, the ground stopped sinking, and I was on solid rock.

Like any good parent, God is more than *willing* to help His children. But unlike any other parent, He possesses the power to meet every challenge, and He's not grieved when you ask. He's grieved when you *fail* to ask. God hates to watch you fall on your face repeatedly, simply because you're too proud to admit you need His help. Have you cried out to God lately? He's waiting.

God not only possesses infinite wisdom and power, He also wants to share them with you.

Day 82: Questions for Reflection

1. Do you generally ask for help?
2. What happens when you ask God for help?
3. What happens when you rely on yourself?
4. Who would you recommend to a friend who needed help?
5. How do you choose to "wait upon the Lord?"
6. How do you imagine God reacts to your requests for help?
7. What do you especially need from God today?

AFFIRMATION 82:

I ask God for everything I need.

Day 83:
Patience

"He who is slow to wrath has great understanding,
but he who is impulsive exalts folly" (Prov. 14:29).

Patience has never come easily to me. Don't get me wrong. I don't sit at stoplights counting the seconds or memorizing the signal pattern. I wait patiently. If only I could keep the rest of my life as calm as this! I need closure, and the sooner I get closure, the better.

Once I start a project, whether it's painting one door or an entire house, I am so driven to finish that I begrudge thirty minutes for lunch. I want the job done well—but quickly. Waiting for the first coat of paint to dry has always frustrated me. My penchant for speed doesn't mean I slop through the job. If I'm not happy with the results, I'll be miserable until I've stripped the paint and started over.

I love to paint because a coat or two produces a vast improvement with minimal investment. If only *personal* improvement were that simple! My old habits refuse to be covered. A dozen coats of the best intentions and fervent resolutions provide only temporary camouflage. Like a persistent grease stain, toxic thinking reappears. When I bought a house with a nasty grease stain over the stove, I reached for KILZ, which seals grease so effectively that the stain will never reappear!

**Repeat the truth over and over until you
overwrite the lies, one at a time.**

Have you tried to strip off your bad habits with no success? What you need is spiritual KILZ, something potent enough to neutralize the old pattern so it will never reappear. The good news is that the Holy Spirit has the power to do just that. The bad news is that He's not in a hurry. Instead of covering up toxic thinking with one coat of truth, He prefers replacement: you repeat the truth over and over until you overwrite the lies, one at a time. This process requires *patience*. Bummers!

When I was in college, my fiancé took a photography class. I liked to tag along when he went into the darkroom to develop his film. There, in the blackness, hidden under developing solution, the nondescript slip of plastic was becoming a thing of beauty. If he pulled it out too soon, there was no image. A little later, the image looked spooky, with hollow eyes and ghost hair. After the process had been allowed its full time with the appropriate solutions and papers, the print emerged, a thing of real beauty.

When nature makes something spectacular, she takes her time. Roses can't be forced open, nor can butterflies be ripped from their cocoons. The God of nature takes His time, too. So, there you are, all yucky, lying in a nasty vat of developer, trusting God. He put you in there when you asked Him to wash away your sin and make you like Him, and He will finish the process.

In the meantime, there's no sense in counting the seconds. The timer will ring at the appropriate time, and His hand will lift you to the light. I pray He will smile, delighted to see His own image smiling back at Him. That moment will be worth all your waiting. In the meantime, PATIENCE!

Day 83: Questions for Reflection

1. When do you feel the most patient?
2. Why do you feel impatient at times?
3. Who brings out your impatience?
4. How patient is God with you?
5. When have you been patient with God?
6. How have you attempted to paint over your bad habits?
7. When will God be finished with you?

AFFIRMATION 83:

I am satisfied to recover slowly or imperfectly.

DAY 84: THANKFUL AND STEADFAST

"And we know that all things work together for good to those who love God, to those who are called according to His purpose" (Rom. 8:28).

Although many Christians quote this scripture, few seem to *believe* it. Most ask God to bless *their* plans, then sink into despair when things go awry. Two years behind his brother in a prestigious private school, my younger son had his sights set on becoming a mechanical engineer. One day toward the end of his junior year, the hapless teen was kicked out of school. Kicked out? My son?!

Didn't God know about the plan? Of course, He did. Apparently, God had a plan of His own. "A man's heart plans his way, but the LORD directs his steps" (Prov. 16:9).

God used my son's misfortune to direct his steps into the medical field, where he served as the best ultrasound technician in the hospital for decades. In other words, God's plans are good.

Had I known the end from the beginning, I would have been praising God for the unnerving turn of events. Lo and behold, God *does* know what He's doing! "Wait a minute," you may say, "God doesn't orchestrate tragedy. It just happens."

Absolutely, but our sovereign Lord is in complete control of all He allows, as the first chapters of the book of Job so poignantly demonstrate. God had a fence around Job, and He allowed Satan to penetrate it only under stringent conditions.

You may be horrified by the extent to which God allowed Satan to harass Job, but God is far more interested in spiritual growth than in prosperity, a fact often overlooked. God, who loves you so much He gave his only Son so you wouldn't perish, won't permit anything that isn't in your best interest.

My husband, one of those disconcerting Christians who truly *believes* God makes all things work together for good, once interrupted my mourning over some seeming tragedy with a hearty, "That's the best thing that could have happened!"

I was taken aback. "You really *believe* all things work together for good?"

"I *used* to believe," he grinned. "Now I *know*."

Knowing is the mark of maturity. When you know, *really* know, in the marrow of your bones, God is on your side, working everything out for your best, you can be at peace, despite your outward circumstances. When the eye of faith perceives God on the throne, you no longer need to understand. Job, perplexed by his tragedies, rued the day he was born. All the while, God had a plan.

God's plan isn't about *you*. He's not in the business of glorifying men. His plan is to glorify Himself, and if you are privileged to have a part in bringing His plan to fulfillment, you, like Job, may experience your share of tragedy. Amazingly, when the plan is finished, and you glimpse God's handiwork, your suffering no longer matters.

Having praised God in his trial, Job ended up with twice as much as he had before, plus ten children, among whom were the three most beautiful women in the land. Because God didn't grant his foolish request to die, Job lived to see his grandchildren to the fourth generation. There's a lot to be said for doggedly refusing to give up! Are you ready to praise God in everything that happens?

I wonder if you, too, have been mistaking the dictator for your conscience.

Day 84: Questions for Reflection

1. What can't you thank God for?
2. How do you react when things don't go your way?
3. Which seeming tragedy turned out to be a blessing?
4. What blessings have you found in horrific losses?
5. Where would you be today if everything had gone as you hoped?
6. How do you understand God's sovereignty?
7. What happens if you praise God for everything?

AFFIRMATION 84:

I never give up.

Day 85:
Perseverance

"Wait on the LORD; Be of good courage. And He shall strengthen your heart; Wait, I say, on the LORD" (Ps. 27:14)!

"Strengthen the hands which hang down, and the feeble knees, and make straight paths for your feet, so that what is lame may not be dislocated, but rather be healed" (Heb. 12:12).

I know more about giving up than I'd like. Not only have I given up on myself, but I have also given up on others. Worse yet, I've watched others give up on themselves. I had known one young man since he was a tyke. Everyone noticed the bright fellow who always knew his lines in the church plays. I taught Steven senior English, where he wrote his term paper on the 1967 Chevelle. The youngest of three boys, he was the first to go to college, worked as a mechanic, and sang in the choir. He even had a girlfriend.

None of us could imagine why this promising youth put a gun in his mouth and pulled the trigger. I went numb when I heard the news. His girlfriend cried all through the funeral. I couldn't stop sobbing. His parents, humble farmers who shared their papayas, couldn't even afford a headstone for his grave. Several times during the week after his funeral, I was sure I saw Steven walking down the street or turning a corner ahead of me. How could such great potential be discarded?

A few years later, a friend of mine gave up on herself. Like most of us, Rosalie had a lot going for her. Despite being able to play the guitar and piano by ear, sing beautifully, compose songs, and paint landscapes, she had decided she had a defect. Had her defect been a hooked nose, I'm confident she would have sought a plastic surgeon, but hers was a secret defect, perhaps imaginary, which no surgery could repair.

I'm not sure *when* she began to feel the hideousness of her handicap outweighing the beauty of her soul. She struggled with depression for years. Perhaps in the end, she was simply too tired to fight anymore. She *was* battling cancer, but those spots on her liver didn't kill her. Giving up did.

The authorities didn't classify Rosalie's death as a suicide, but because she left a note, they did require an autopsy. Her husband told me she died of pneumonia. The note she left made it clear she was aware she might not survive the night and chose not to seek medical attention. Her illness provided a clean way out, but the aftermath was horrific. Those close to her agonized, *Why didn't I notice?*

I still think of my friend: her dreams to travel, her desire to pray her relatives into the kingdom, and her yearning to make cute wall hangings for the grandchildren she hoped to have. She wanted to own a horse again. She had so much to live for. If only she hadn't given up.

Giving up may seem like the easiest way out of a dilemma or even the right way, but giving up is never the best way. If you don't remember anything else I've written, please remember this: NEVER GIVE UP!

If you don't remember anything else, please remember this: NEVER GIVE UP!

Day 85: Questions for Reflection

1. How many times have you felt like giving up?
2. What makes your life worth living?
3. How do you feel about those who have given up?
4. Who has given up on himself but is still alive?
5. What would make you give up on yourself?
6. When have you felt God had given up on you?
7. How do you know God will never give up on you?

AFFIRMATION 85:

I thank God for everything that happens.

Day 86:
Forgiveness

"For if you forgive men their trespasses, your heavenly Father will also forgive you" (Matt. 6:14).

Forgiveness is easy when the offense is slight. A stranger may step on your toe and bump a package out of your arms, causing pain and inconvenience. You forgive him because he had no intention to harm you. Accidents happen, and fussing over them spoils an otherwise lovely day. Should your package, however, contain a rare antique that shatters upon impact, forgiveness becomes more challenging. Most of you would still pardon the oaf. But what if the stranger worked for a competing antique store? Would you call the police? Intent to harm is a key ingredient.

What about those times when the offense was not only premeditated, but cruel, and the perpetrator is not some stranger, but a friend, lover, or even a parent? When my husband was five, his mother beat him so severely that he lay in bed for three days. Abuse of this caliber is not a minor inconvenience, but a trauma that twists the psyche, deadening spontaneity and joy. Forgiving such offenses is complicated. Could God really require us to forgive *everything*?

One morning, I was sitting at the kitchen table with my Bible when I sensed my heavenly Father saying, "Today, instead of reading My word, I'd like you to write a letter to your stepfather."

Is there someone you need to forgive?

My stomach sank. I hadn't spoken to my stepfather in years. Surely God understood how painful communicating with that man would be. I shivered at the thought of the task and tried to beg off.

"That would be hard for me."

His voice was gentle. "I've done some hard things for you."

Bursting into tears, I pulled out a sheet of paper. What I wrote on it was not pleasant. I wanted to mention that the young daughters from his second marriage had been molested because what goes around comes around! I didn't, but the missive was still too bitter to mail. I had to write that letter three times before I dared to place it in an envelope. Only then did I discover I didn't have the man's address! God had asked me to write that letter because *I* needed to forgive.

What about you, my friend? Are there offenses you've stockpiled? Is there someone you need to forgive? A letter you need to write, even if you don't know your abuser's address or if they are deceased? You're not forgiving for their sakes. You're cutting the chain that has bound you to the traumas of your past. Forgiveness is God's way to break free, and your freedom is well worth the price.

Day 86: Questions for Reflection

1. How easily do you forgive?
2. How important is intent to harm?
3. Who do you need to forgive?
4. How many have wronged you?
5. What prevents you from forgiving everyone?
6. How serious is God about you forgiving evildoers?
7. Is forgiving the same as forgetting?

AFFIRMATION 86:

I forgive all who have hurt me.

Day 87:
Forgiving My Enemies

"But I say to you, love your enemies, bless those
who curse you, do good to those who hate you,
and pray for those who spitefully use you
and persecute you" (Matt. 5:44).

"*The Passion of the Christ* changed my life," a man in my Bible study remarked, "especially the scene in which Jesus pleads with His Father to forgive His tormentors."

Having seen the brutality Christ endured, the viewer was overwhelmed. That scene encapsulates the spirit of the Savior: forgiveness freely offered, regardless of the affront. But Jesus offered more than *His* forgiveness; He prayed that *God* would forgive them as well.

Christians often express a desire to be like Jesus, believing they need to perform more good deeds. Unfortunately, many who excel in good deeds fall short in the most Christ-like characteristic, asking God to forgive their tormentors. Without this step, forgiveness is phony. We may *say* we forgive while thinking, *Okay, you schmuck, I'll let you off the hook, but I can't wait to see how God pays you back.* This is not forgiveness. The "forgiver" hasn't let go of the offense. He's simply postponed the payback.

King David gives us an example of delayed payback. When he returned to Jerusalem after the death of Absalom, the son who had attempted to seize his throne, he seemed to pardon Shimei, the filthy-mouthed man who had cursed him as he fled. But on his deathbed, David instructed his recently-crowned son, King Solomon, *not* to allow Shimei to die a natural death. David hadn't forgotten. He'd simply postponed the day of vengeance.

Jesus's pardon goes beyond overlooking the offense. He actually *blesses* the perpetrator. While Solomon advised his readers to do good to their enemies, Jesus commanded you to pray for those who spitefully use you. God knows this isn't humanly possible. Perhaps that's why He said the world would know you were a Christian by your love. When others see you forgiving as Jesus did, they recognize the heart of God. Do you *really* want to be like Jesus? Pray for those who misuse you.

One pastor's wife was determined to fast for a week until she was able to forgive her stepfather for the abuse that had robbed her of her childhood. In the middle of the week, when he knocked on her door, a wave of love flowed through her. God had answered her prayers, and He will do the same for you if you seek Him with the same earnestness.

God wants you to go to bed with every offense forgiven, every day. What's in it for you? The joy of obedience and intimacy with God, plus fellowship with others. If forgiveness sounds like a challenge, try praying for the person who hurt you. You may be surprised. Some of my worst enemies have become my best friends.

God wants you to go to bed with every offense forgiven–every day.

Day 87: Questions for Reflection:

1. What grudge have you held?
2. How does God want you to relate to your abusers?
3. How successful are you in forgiving?
4. When have you prayed for an abuser?
5. What was the result of your prayer?
6. How does God's justice relate to forgiving others?
7. How do you benefit by interceding for your abusers?

AFFIRMATION 87:

I ask God to forgive all who have hurt me.

Day 88:
Forgiving God

"But it displeased Jonah exceedingly,
and he became angry" (Jonah 4:1).

Few of us admit we're angry with God, but if we were honest, we might find most of the church holding a grudge against Him. I have a friend who's fond of joking, "There is a God, and I'm not Him."

That quip never fails to elicit a laugh, perhaps because we've all experienced this familiar feeling: *I alone, among all the billions on Earth, know the right thing to do at any moment. If only others would consult me and follow my instructions. Alas! They have their own ideas.*

When someone disagrees with me, I console myself that the poor fellow doesn't know any better. How could he? He isn't me! Because he's too foolish to listen to my opinion, there is little hope he'll demonstrate good sense.

But when the One with the opposing opinion is God, my rationalizations dissolve like powdered Jell-O in a stream of boiling water. After all, God is the all-knowing, Almighty One who does whatever He wants, and I suddenly realize I am not. When God topples my childish ideas like a baby's tower of blocks, I want to cry.

Sure, God knows what's best, and He never makes a mistake. Does that mean I always agree with Him? If I were to be honest, I'd have to admit I sometimes feel angry with God. There are times when He seems to side with my enemies. At least, theirs are the plans that are prospering, not mine. Either God hasn't heard me, or He has ignored me. How am I supposed to feel about that?

You will have to forgive God for smashing those precious dreams that stood between you and Him.

How do *you* respond when God allows circumstances you deplore? A knee-jerk reaction of annoyance? *Why on Earth did You permit that?* A pouting withdrawal? *I'll just take my ball and go home.* A fist-shaking tirade. *You must hate me as much as I hate You.*

You might be surprised to know that God would rather have you say any of those things than say nothing at all. Sure, I know forgiving God seems ridiculous. He's never done anything wrong. Yet, when the heat of disappointment creeps up your cheeks, you know you're feeling wronged. Unless and until you release those feelings, anger will rule you.

Let's ask Job how he dealt with his conviction that God was mistaken in allowing so much misfortune to decimate him. In lengthy, eloquent speeches, he challenged God to answer his questions, yet God found no fault in Job's audacious words. When the Almighty showed up to ask Job some questions of His own, He defended His servant.

God said Job had spoken what was right about Him. He was pleased with Job's attempt to make sense of his disaster. By the way, did you notice Job was healed *after* he prayed for his friends—the ones who had accused him of being a sinner? As God forgave him, he forgave them, and then he reaped the consequences, a harvest of healing.

When I studied flying, I learned how dangerous a spin can be. As you descend in a tight little spiral, the forces become violent enough to tear off the wings, so it's essential to get out as quickly as possible. How? Apply the opposite rudder. In this case, opposite rudder means to jump out of your ivory tower and admit that God knows best.

There is a God, and you're not Him. Relax, brain. You don't have to know the answer to every problem. Relax, body. You don't have to be in control of every circumstance. God is fully capable, eternally vigilant, all-wise, and all-loving. You may not understand His ways, but He doesn't ask you to understand. He asks you to trust and obey.

In order to do that, you will have to forgive God for smashing those precious dreams that stood between you and Him. You will have to honor Him with the sacrifice of praise. Yes, even when you can't find a single reason to be grateful.

Follow the advice of James, the Lord's brother: thank Him *in* the mess. Rest assured, He's using it to paint a picture of His face on your heart. After all, isn't that what you asked? As for Jonah, the angry prophet in today's scripture, he never tells us whether he chose to forgive God or not. I hope he did, and I hope you will.

God already knows how you feel. He sees through the poker face you wear. Are you afraid to write God a letter for fear of other people reading your journal? Job's was published in the best-selling book of all time and circulated around the world for thousands of years!

God welcomes your expressions of anger. When you tell Him your disappointments, He'll take you in His arms and soothe your pain.

Day 88: Questions for Reflection

1. When was the last time you felt angry with God?
2. How did you express your anger?
3. When is being angry with God okay?
4. What does God know about your emotions?
5. Who suffers when you hold a grudge?
6. What happens when you forgive God?
7. When will you forgive God for disappointing you?

AFFIRMATION 88:

I forgive God for disappointing me.

DAY 89:
WOUNDING MYSELF

"There is a way that seems right to a man,
but its end is the way of death" (Prov. 14:12).

When Moses told Pharaoh that God had sent him to lead His people into the wilderness for worship, Pharaoh laughed—at least inwardly. He'd have saved himself great loss if he'd listened, but "gods" don't listen. *Imagine slaves demanding a holiday! Preposterous!* Such thinking cost him his drinking water, his crops, his cattle, the lives of his servants, untold misery, and eventually, his firstborn son.

How could anyone continue to fight God after such an unbroken string of defeats? Moses tells us. God hardened Pharaoh's heart. "And I will harden Pharaoh's heart, and multiply My signs and My wonders in the land of Egypt" (Exodus 7:3).

Seems clear, doesn't it?

But in Exodus 8:32, we read something quite different. "But Pharaoh hardened his heart at this time also; neither would he let the people go."

I'm confused, aren't you? I don't claim to comprehend the delicate interplay between the sovereignty of God and the free will of man. What I *do* understand is that we *all* have choices. We can *choose* to harden our hearts. Pharaoh did.

Are you attempting to manipulate God into giving you your desires?

How could the political and spiritual head of the greatest nation of his time make such a foolish decision? Pharaoh thought *he* was god. Why should the manifestation of deity on Earth listen to the God of a ragged band of slaves? Bolstered by his magicians' duplication of God's first two signs, he continued to harden his heart.

Then the sorcerers failed, unable to create lice. "Then the magicians said to Pharaoh, 'This is the finger of God.' But Pharaoh's heart grew hard, and he did not heed them, just as the LORD had said" (Exod. 8:19).

Fast forward five plagues to the aftermath of the eighth, when crops and cattle were gone. "Then Pharaoh's servants said to him, 'How long shall this man be a snare to us? Let the men go, that they may serve the LORD their God. Do you not yet know that Egypt is destroyed'" (Exod. 10:7)?

He knew. He didn't care. He couldn't bow to the wishes of Jehovah and still be god himself. So he dragged an entire nation through ten plagues: blood, frogs, lice, flies, livestock disease, boils, hail, locusts, darkness, and death!

I do the same on a much smaller scale, and so do you. God makes it plain: He alone is almighty. We are not. We are erring humans struggling against all-too-common foibles that sometimes get the best of us. How easily we slip into Pharaoh's folly, parading ourselves as though we were somebodies and putting others in harm's way to protect our false identities. Like Pharaoh, we can't bow to God while trying to be God ourselves. We hate to admit we make mistakes, get sick, or need help. We advise others but never need advice. Rubbish! And worse than rubbish—idolatry!

Who is the Lord of your life? Are you attempting to manipulate God into giving you your desires? (Begging leads to a great deal of pouting, foot stomping, and angry squeals when you don't get what you want.) Or are you working to give God what *He* wants? The heart set on God is filled with the joy of the Lord and gratitude to be called to suffer for Him. There is no one you've failed to forgive, not even yourself. You are slow to give advice and quick to listen, especially to the still, small voice of God's Spirit.

Many think God's path leads to a rose garden. Joseph's led to a prison, Daniel's to a lion's den, the baptizer's to a chopping block, but none of that matters when you're truly surrendered. Are you ready to admit: There is a God, and I'm not Him?

Day 89: Questions for Reflection

1. Who do you need to forgive?
2. How much do you expect of yourself?
3. Who do you really worship?
4. How easily do you take advice?
5. When have you hardened your heart?
6. What needs to change for you to listen to God?
7. How have you tried to play god yourself?

AFFIRMATION 89:

I ask forgiveness for every wrong I've done.

DAY 90:
GOD'S FORGIVENESS

"For You, Lord, are good, and ready to forgive, And abundant in mercy to all those who call upon You" (Ps. 86:5).

I've read that men should give their wives flowers rather than a potted plant because a woman views a plant as something to care for, while she sees flowers as something to enjoy and discard. I've always preferred plants, partly because I feel guilty about receiving a pricey gift that lasts only a few days.

Anita, a friend from Germany, shares my sentiments. She told her husband never to buy her flowers. Unfortunately, the friends in Germany with whom they spent their fiftieth wedding anniversary hadn't heard. "They gave us fifty red roses," Anita grimaced. "I had to smile and look happy, but I wished they hadn't done that."

I've experienced the same feelings. Have you?

Given the comment, "For me? That's gorgeous!" many of us immediately imagine the following line: "I couldn't possibly accept such an expensive gift."

There are several potential reasons for our discomfort, not the least of which is the awful feeling of being indebted to the giver for the amount of the gift. I suspect a worse culprit is the nagging doubt that we are worth the expense.

Jesus knew how to receive an expensive gift with grace. Shortly before His crucifixion, Mary of Bethany poured an alabaster box of exquisite perfume, valued at a year's wages, onto His head. As the fragrance of sweet spikenard announced the extravagant gesture, the disciples recoiled. *What a waste!* They were calculating what they would rather have done with the money, while Jesus was appreciating an act of love so intense it demanded the best. He set His disciples straight.

"'Why do you trouble the woman? For she has done a good work for Me . . . . Assuredly, I say to you, wherever this gospel is preached in the whole world, what this woman has done will also be told as a memorial to her'" (Matt. 26:10,13).

Jesus, the sinless Son of God, deserved the costly oil. I'm sure you agree. But when God offers *you* forgiveness, which cost the agonizing death of His only Son, you may balk, at least inwardly, feeling unworthy. No stretch of your imagination can justify lavishing heaven's treasure on you. Yet, that's what God did, and He won't take it back. Like the fragrant oil from the alabaster flask, the lifeblood of the Son of God has already been poured out—for you.

Refusing the forgiveness Christ purchased insults Him. Today, quiet the babble of voices calling the gift excessive by agreeing. *Yes, this gift is unthinkably extravagant. I can never hope to deserve God's forgiveness or fully appreciate what Jesus did for me. All I can do is praise Him for His sacrifice. Thank you, Jesus.*

You will never be able to repay your debt, but you don't need to. You've been forgiven; the record of your sins has been completely blotted out. God does not expect you to reciprocate with anything except your love. Let your spirit soar. Jesus is LORD.

You have been forgiven; the record of your sins has been completely blotted out.

Day 90: Questions for Reflection

1. When were you hesitant to accept a gift?
2. How can you accept expensive gifts with grace?
3. Do you care how much your gifts cost?
4. Who really deserves God's forgiveness?
5. How could you become worthy of His pardon?
6. What prevents you from accepting God's forgiveness?
7. Which extravagant gifts have you received from God?

AFFIRMATION 90:

I accept God's forgiveness.

Day 91:
Forgiving Myself

"There is therefore now no condemnation to those who are in Christ Jesus, who do not walk according to the flesh, but according to the Spirit" (Rom. 8:1).

This morning, I listened to the director of the local mission tell of an alcoholic who fell asleep in bed with a lit cigarette. The resultant fire burned Tom's arm, but he was too drunk to realize he'd been injured until three days later. By then, gangrene had set in, and doctors were forced to amputate. How could anyone fail to realize he was in so much pain?

I could feel Tom's despair when he realized the price of his carelessness. The experience sobered him. The following year, he moved, gave up alcohol, got engaged, and became a successful businessman. If he hadn't forgiven himself, he might still be an alcoholic. I salute his courage, and I laud his self-forgiveness. Forgiving oneself isn't easy.

You know holding a grudge is damaging, but when the person you're angry with is yourself, you suffer twice the harm. Failing to forgive yourself makes as much sense as failing to seek medical attention for a severe burn. Do you love to scold yourself because it feels good to take out your bottled-up rage on a safe target? You may think no one else gets hurt, but in reality, everyone suffers. You deprive your family of the cheer you could be spreading. You are a dark cloud at work, and your friends miss the loving support you could provide if you weren't so busy putting yourself down.

How do you forgive yourself? Begin with a decision to stop the punishment. Paul said there is no condemnation for those in Christ Jesus. None! The King of the Universe has forgiven you and given you a new position in His royal family. "Beloved, now are we children of God" (1 John 3:2). Stop and think. How should you treat God's precious child?

Once we forgive ourselves, we are willing to let others help us.

My husband, who has a great aversion to doctors, fell off a machine in the Yavapai College weight room and passed out. When he regained consciousness, bellowing like a wounded buffalo, he refused medical attention. A week later, at the insistence of his teacher, he submitted to X-rays, which revealed four broken ribs. I want to think he would have dialed 911 if I had been the one injured. I suspect many of us treat others better than we treat ourselves.

In our fantasies, you and I would all like to be Superman, and we're bitterly disappointed when our attempts to "leap tall buildings in a single bound" land us in the hospital instead of the clouds. Give up pretending. Forgive yourself for being human. You're in good company. Christopher Reeve, who played Superman, spent the last ten years of his life in a wheelchair after a fall from a horse.

Join me around an imaginary campfire, telling tales of the seemingly impossible undertakings you've tackled. Sometimes you flopped. Sometimes you succeeded. Sometimes you succeeded and paid the price for years. When he was seventy-eight but thought he was still eighteen, my husband insisted on pushing an evaporative cooler up a ladder onto the roof—by himself.

As soon as he reached the top, the neighbor spotted him. "Do you need help?"

"No, thank you!"

The damage was done. Already suffering from thin vertebrae due to osteoporosis, he had compressed his fragile spine. Medical tests showed delayed nerve response in his legs, irreversible damage worsened by the arthritis and scoliosis he'd contended with for years.

I don't pretend to understand his thinking, but I know one important fact: Once we forgive ourselves, we drop our pretense of being Superman and are willing to let others help us. Forgive yourself for being human. You'll enjoy the results.

Day 91: Questions for Reflection

1. What do you expect of yourself but no one else?
2. How realistic are your expectations?
3. When do you treat yourself cruelly?
4. In what ways do you attempt to be Superman?
5. What happens when you disappoint yourself?
6. Which grudges are you holding against yourself?
7. Why haven't you forgiven yourself?

AFFIRMATION 91:

I forgive myself.

Day 92:
Thank God I'm Alive

"But for him who is joined to all the living there is hope, for a living dog is better than a dead lion" (Eccles. 9:4).

This morning, I happened on a nasty accident five minutes from home. From the number of emergency vehicles on the scene, this was more than a fender bender. We're not supposed to rubberneck, but if you're like me, you can't help peeking. I cast a furtive glance at the smashed blue pickup as the policeman motioned me through the intersection.

From the looks of the badly crumpled passenger door, someone could have died at the intersection of Cornville Road and Highway 89A on this lovely spring morning, someone who woke up dreaming of cinnamon raisin bagels and cream cheese, someone with no intention of being tucked into a coffin before sunset.

Having recently been involved in a fender bender, I drove away realizing I had missed being in the wrong place at the wrong time by minutes. On an average day, any one of us could meet an untimely demise on the highway, victims of our own poor judgment or the runaway adrenaline of someone else's road rage. Yet most of us pass smoothly through day after day unscathed, though we can point to moments when we *almost* died.

As a child, I rubbed elbows with death when I slipped off an inner tube and sank to the bottom of a swimming pool. Mother, perched on the diving board, immediately leaped in and fished me out. My baby brother had his brush with an untimely end when an ice cube lodged in his throat and blocked his airway. Although Mother upended him and pounded on his back, he was turning blue. In desperation, she rammed her finger down his throat, where the tip of a long red nail tilted the ice cube enough to allow the air to flow.

This afternoon, I stood at the bedside of a friend. Two months ago, she went in for surgery. Today she lies still, eyes closed, her hand taped with intravenous needles, tightly grasping mine. I sing to her. Sometimes she smiles, but more often her white lips are pressed into a straight line. After two hours, she forces her eyes open and releases my hand. "You've done enough," she says. "Go home and rest."

Wouldn't you like to become fully human and fully alive?

I straighten my stiff back. In the hall, I speak with her sister. "It must have been the chemo. She went downhill fast after they started the second round. All she wants now is to go home to her puppies. The hospice workers have agreed to take her tomorrow—if she survives the night."

The sliding glass doors of the hospital open automatically. I step into the cool, windy evening, my senses overwhelmed by the fragrance of juniper, the warm breath of the wind, and the saltiness of my tears. I am alive, and for a moment, I am truly thankful for the incomparable gift of life.

As you tumble out of bed, intent on your routine, how alive are you? Do you notice the warmth of the sun on your skin or the soothing aroma of morning coffee? Or do you stumble through life like the living dead, head down, full steam ahead? Push! Work! Accomplish! What happened to live, love, and enjoy? Ask yourself what's really important. Being truly alive allows you to be intimately connected to God and your fellow man. Wouldn't you like to become fully human and fully alive?

Day 92: Questions for Reflection

1. Do you remember any narrow escapes as a child?
2. How many times have you been in near-death situations?
3. To what do you attribute your survival?
4. How thankful are you to be alive?
5. What have you done to celebrate your life?
6. How often do you express your thanks to God?
7. What specific events remind you to be thankful?

AFFIRMATION 92:

I am thankful to be alive.

Day 93:
Alone and Lonely

"A man who isolates himself seeks his own desire;
He rages against all wise judgment" (Prov. 18:1).

On March 10, 1975, the world was shocked to discover World War II was still being fought, albeit on a very small scale. A lone Japanese foot soldier, Lieutenant Hiroo Onoda, was still at his post on Lubang, a tiny island in the Philippines, where he had been sent in 1944 to spy on American forces. Refusing to believe Japan had surrendered, Onoda had remained stubbornly faithful to a duty which no longer existed.

For over three decades, he had lived off the land, subsisting on what he could forage from the jungle or steal from local farmers. A proud man dedicated to an impossible mission, Onoda couldn't relinquish his dream. What was he thinking during those solitary decades? Did he consider surrender? Had he invested too much to risk losing face? Whatever the case, Lt. Onoda remained at war for more than thirty years after the end of hostilities.

His story haunts me, perhaps because I, too, have found surrender almost impossible. I suspect I am not the only one. Since Eve reached for the forbidden fruit, mankind has struggled against surrender. When you are honest with yourself, do you discover that in your heart of hearts, you don't really want God's plans; you want your own? Like the last combatant in World War II, you may cling to your dreams, mindlessly pursuing a course of action doomed to failure.

What does it take to awaken a self-deluded soldier from his trance? A reality check. For Lt. Onoda, that reality check came in the form of a visit from the man who had once served as his commanding officer. Onoda went home. He mastered the grueling transition from guerrilla fighter to Average Joe Citizen, opened a nature park for children, and became a successful businessman.

According to a CNN article posted on May 26, 1996, twenty years after the end of his exile, Onoda returned to Lubang, where he surrendered his sword to Ferdinand Marcos, then president of the Philippines, and thanked the island people, presenting them with a ten-thousand-dollar check for children's scholarships.

I have much to learn from Lt. Onoda. I, too, have wasted decades entrapped by false ideas; in my case, the hope that perfection would bring acceptance. Now that you can see the lie in that false hope, will you join me in surrendering your pride, embracing reality, and admitting your best efforts can never make you perfect? Today, I choose to crawl out of my foxhole and make the painful transition to everyday life, and I'm hoping you'll be right there with me. And yes, I am finally willing to accept God's plans.

Have you wondered whether you are living in the real world or a virtual reality? How can you tell the difference with virtual realities becoming so realistic? Even those around you may be fooled, so you need input from God. Without His help, the devil may sell you a bill of goods leading to the bottomless pit. When you seek the Lord, He will show you the straight and narrow way.

Have you wondered whether you are living in the real world or a virtual reality?

Day 93: Questions for Reflection

1. Which painful illusions have entrapped you?
2. What keeps you from acknowledging the truth?
3. What would your reality check look like?
4. How easily could you make the transition to reality?
5. In what ways is your story similar to Mr. Onoda's?
6. In what ways is your story different?
7. Under what circumstances could you accept God's plans?

AFFIRMATION 93:

I accept God's plans for my life.

Day 94:
Who Am I?

"But you are a chosen generation, a royal priest-
hood, a holy nation, His own special people, that
you may proclaim the praises of Him who called
you out of darkness into His marvelous light"
(1 Pet. 2:9).

When I read Shakespeare's play *Julius Caesar*, I found an interesting line in Act II, Scene 2. "Cowards die a thousand deaths, but the valiant taste of death but once." Hmmm.

I had never wanted to think of myself as a coward, but I knew I was. Those thousand deaths were my life story. Fear stalked me at every turn. I rationalized that the coward's deaths were little ones, which might save me from the gargantuan death of the valiant. I was wrong.

In my zeal to avoid pain, I had relegated myself to the ranks of the walking dead. For years, I passed unnoticed among the living like a shadow, hearing their laughter as though from a distance, separated from life by an invisible shield. I didn't want to be real, not if being real meant being vulnerable.

An insulating numbness protects those fearful of self-disclosure. Their invisible shields dampen emotions, yet many who live in this semi-anesthetized state haven't noticed. It's all they know. Is this your story? Have you observed others savoring seasons and rhythms of life you scarcely detect? Do you feel disconnected, as though a glass stands between you and the real world?

In *The Velveteen Rabbit* by Margery Williams, the Skin Horse explains the cost of becoming real: your eyes drop out; most of your hair is rubbed off; you become shabby. The price is high. Opening your heart to love brings pain, but life will no longer pass you by. You will be real.

As for me, I choose to awaken from my stupor. No longer will seasons pass without my notice or daisies bloom in vain along my pathway. Today I will breathe in the sweet fragrance of freshly mowed grass, feel the warmth of the sun on my skin, and hear the quaint two-syllable cry of the quail. I will watch the wild oats bend their heads in the breeze and know I, too, can bend before the wind and stand upright again when the tempest has passed.

I embrace the messiness of being human, welcoming the good and the bad, the happy and the sad, as necessary parts of life. I welcome myself, too; a self who will never be fully known, with all my follies and foibles, my virtues and vices, my past and my present, as well as my future. I refuse to hide in the shadows, ashamed because I don't have life figured out. No one does. Those who seem so sure of themselves are only pretending. Like you and me, they are fellow travelers on the journey of life.

Do you feel disconnected, as though a glass stands between you and the real world?

For some, the journey has to become unbearable before they are willing to change. The phone roused me from a deep sleep this morning, but the energy in the voice on the other end quickly swept away the cobwebs. Unable to bear the pain of his past, Bob had slit his wrists a few days earlier. When his desperate attempt to take his life had failed, he had decided to change course. He'd stopped running, stopped medicating, and started living. Bob had called to announce he was putting down his invisible shield to become vulnerable. His valor made me cry.

As we talked, I learned that, like me, my friend had failed to live up to his mother's expectations. Like me, his feelings had not been validated. Today, we acknowledged the pain he'd felt when he was molested so he could leave the past behind and become real.

Bob now wants to work for a living, to cry when he's sad, and to rage when he's angry instead of snorting cocaine. Not everyone will rejoice. Real people threaten zombies, but the strong zombies who use their minds to deaden their emotions and the weak zombies who resort to drugs or alcohol need real people to awaken them. Congratulations, Bob! Happy birthday! Enjoy your new life.

Where do you fit into this picture? You may think you're fully alive and aware of the wonderful world about you when you're really only half here. If you've identified with the concept of being unmindful of the world around you to any degree, I invite you to search for the path to vibrant life. Once you are fully awake and alive, you'll be surprised at how much you've been missing.

Day 94: Questions for Reflection

1. How fully do you participate in life's rhythms?
2. Which parts of life have you missed?
3. How often do you medicate your pain?
4. What is your drug of choice?
5. Where can you fully acknowledge your past and present?
6. Are you able to participate in the joys and sorrows of others?
7. What does being a real person entail?

AFFIRMATION 94:

I am discovering who I am.

Day 95:
No Superman

"For you see your calling, brethren, that not many
wise according to the flesh, not many mighty,
not many noble, are called" (1 Cor. 1:26).

In 1996, doctors told Lance Armstrong, a world-class cyclist, that his testicular cancer had spread to his lungs and brain. They removed a testicle, subjected him to months of chemotherapy, and gave him a 40 percent chance of survival. The Texan not only survived, but he also accomplished what few dream of doing. Within a few years, he was winning the prestigious Tour de France. On July 25, 2004, Armstrong, one of the five-member "Club of Five" riders who had taken the Tour de France five times, became the first man in history to win the grueling race for the sixth time.

Armstrong wanted to be Superman. He didn't even let testicular cancer devastate his family plans. After receiving his second Tour de France trophy, he lifted his nine-month-old son, Luke, over his head. He had taken the precaution to freeze his sperm before chemotherapy, and the boy was later conceived in a test tube. He had two more children with his first wife and won more races.

Then this world-famous athlete spent ten years denying he had taken performance-enhancing drugs, until the US Anti-Doping Agency formally charged him. In 2013, he came clean to Oprah Winfrey. Yes, he'd used testosterone, human growth hormone, EPO, and blood transfusions. He was stripped of his Tour de France wins and Olympic medals, and today we remember him as the man who cheated.

Few people have the discipline to train for the Tour de France, and fewer still have the resilience to overcome brain cancer. Armstrong did both. Why did he feel the need to cheat? He wasn't satisfied to be merely human. He needed to be Superman.

Contrast him with Gail Devers, a five-time Olympic gold medalist who's been called the fastest woman in the world. She became so ill after her first Olympic Games that she dropped from 125 to eighty-seven pounds and lost most of her hair. For two years, she suffered from severe fatigue and a rapid heart rate. Doctors were discussing amputating her leg when Graves' disease was finally diagnosed, and her thyroid was treated with radioactive iodine.

With both legs intact, she recovered to win additional Olympic gold medals. Without relying on performance-enhancing drugs, Devers did her best with the gifts God had given her. She later spoke on Capitol Hill and is the champion of those suffering from thyroid disease. She shares her story so others will think, *If she survived, I can too.*

I grew up on stories of superheroes who could ski their way to victory on a wooden leg. I was awed by Beethoven, who didn't let his deafness get in the way of writing symphonies. Fanny Crosby composed an astounding number of hymns and carried on a worldwide speaking ministry despite being blind. My illogical conclusion: *since I can see and hear, I should do even greater things.*

Have you lived an ordinary life like me?

We all have people to measure up to: siblings, aunts, uncles, and grandparents, some of whom distinguished themselves as legislators, actors, or scientists. Some of us wanted to write our names in a hall of fame. A few of us will, but what about the rest of us?

Have you distinguished yourself, or have you lived an ordinary life like mine? I studied hard, earned good grades, and held two or three jobs. On the side, I wrote songs. I doubt I'll ever be famous, but I'd be happy if my CDs helped one person recover from the lies they've believed, or if this book rescued one soul from the pit. I'm as common as 99 percent of the people I know. How about you? Wouldn't you rather go down in history as an ordinary person than a famous cheater?

Day 95: Questions for Reflection

1. Who were the heroes of your childhood?
2. What aspirations of greatness have you nurtured?
3. What did your family expect of you?
4. What expectations have you held for yourself?
5. In which aspects of your life are you a superstar?
6. In which aspects of your life are you ordinary?
7. Why do you need to distinguish yourself?

AFFIRMATION 95:

I am willing to be an ordinary person.

DAY 96: OVERCOMERS

"And he said: 'Naked I came from my mother's
womb, And naked shall I return there.
The LORD gave, and the LORD has taken away;
Blessed be the name of the LORD'" (Job 1:21).

The Bible recounts the story of Job, the wealthiest man of his time, who fell from riches to rags in one heartbreaking day. Since he declined to curse God after losing every asset *and* his ten children, the devil then deprived him of his health. For most of the book, Job, who is described as "blameless and upright, a man who fears God and shuns evil," sits in an ash heap scraping his boils and feeling miserable enough to lament the day he was born.

Despite his friends' innuendos that he is hiding a grievous sin, and his wife's advice that he curse God and die, Job survives his fiery ordeal. In the last chapter, God blesses him with double the goods he had and ten more children. Job passed his horrific test with honors. Some of us who fail far less strenuous tests are anxious to know his secret.

Because the book of Job doesn't have a neat moral tacked onto the end, the reader is left to dig for the secret to Job's resilience. I found one tucked into the middle of the book, where a beleaguered Job tells his grief counselors, "But He knows the way that I take; When He has tested me, I shall come forth as gold" (Job 23:10). In my mind, the entire forty-two chapters find their footing in this sterling declaration.

Job overcame in part because he *expected* to overcome, and he expected to overcome because the God he served was good. When friends and family were focused on the details of his disaster, Job had eyes for God's heavens, lips to declare His goodness, and a heart full of the certainty that the God who does "whatever His soul desires" (Job 23:13) would one day complete Job's testing and bring him forth, refined to shine like pure gold.

If Job's were the only victory-over-tragedy story in the Bible, we might brush it off, but the fourth chapter of Daniel records an amazingly similar tale. The legendary King Nebuchadnezzar, potentate of Babylon, the ruling empire on Earth, was troubled by a dream of a huge tree cut to a stump and banded with iron and bronze so it could grow again. As Daniel explained, the king himself was the tree.

A year later, Nebuchadnezzar began to boast of his accomplishments, immediately became insane, and was driven from the palace. He then lived as a wild animal for seven years, eating grass until his nails grew like bird claws. This heathen king fell further than Job, but when his reason returned, he was restored to his kingdom and enjoyed *added*, excellent majesty.

How did Nebuchadnezzar survive the culture shock of going from the most powerful position on Earth to the least powerful in less time than it takes to type the question mark at the end of this sentence? I suspect Daniel's assurance that the cut-down tree would one day grow again sustained the monarch. He had God's promise that in due time he would flourish. Like Job, he expected to overcome.

What do you expect? If God could rescue Job from the brink of death and Nebuchadnezzar from the depths of insanity, He can deliver you. Have you asked Him? Once you do, begin expecting to overcome.

**God can deliver you. Have you asked Him?
Once you do, begin expecting to overcome.**

Day 96: Questions for Reflection

1. When did you expect to overcome an obstacle?
2. How has willpower helped you change old habits?
3. When has God helped you to overcome?
4. How can God be trusted to strengthen you?
5. What difference does the assurance of victory make?
6. What are God's intentions toward you?
7. How do you expect to overcome perfectionism?

AFFIRMATION 96:

I overcome every obstacle.

Day 97:
Perfect Peace

"Peace I leave with you, My peace I give to you;
not as the world gives do I give to you. Let not
your heart be troubled, neither let it be afraid"
(John 14:27).

Have you wondered what emotions Noah experienced as he stepped off the ark? Peace would not be my first guess. After seven hours sailing from Molokai to Oahu on a forty-foot ketch in small craft warnings, I was ecstatic to step onto dry land and quiet my queasy stomach. Noah had been in the ark for over a year. A long year!

When the boat rested on the Mountains of Ararat and the Earth was finally dry, Noah released a dove, his version of a reconnaissance drone. She returned the second day with an olive branch in her beak. A dove with an olive branch has become a worldwide symbol of peace. The war is over. Arise and rebuild. The God-honoring loyalists ventured forth to begin anew.

There are days I identify with Noah; I feel as though *my* world has been destroyed. I wanted to be perfect, but with a single blast of His nostrils, God scattered my hopes to the four winds. Now there is only turbulence, and I feel as though I'm drifting with no way to steer my tiny craft. Worse, my efforts to attain perfection have driven me away from the One who is willing to pour His perfection into my surrendered life.

Wait! Did I just hint there's hope? Yes, but the keyword is "surrendered." The only thing God can do with a rebellious heart is send sufficient trouble to awaken the owner of that heart to his peril.

"God," have you prayed, "I know what I want isn't your first choice, but if You let me do things my way, You'll be happy with the results." Do you suppose that's what Eve was thinking when she eyed the tree of the knowledge of good and evil? Doing things her way didn't turn out well for her, and your way won't turn out well for you either.

If you operate *within* the will of God and you actually live *in* Christ, you will partake of the same peace that sustained Jesus through the cross. Dwelling in the center of God's will, you'll discover how little perplexes you. What does it matter if you are no longer beautiful—or never were? You do not need to dazzle others with wealth or wisdom. You no longer desire more stuff. Your focus is on rendering perfect obedience to your sovereign Lord.

As for Noah, I think he stepped out of the ark bravely. God had told him to go in a year earlier. Now God was telling him to come out. He took each step as God revealed it, and that's all God asks of you. But God does more than ask. He promises to reward you if you obey. Noah received a rainbow as a promise of no further floods. You have a more precious promise, peace in the midst of your floods.

Have you spent your life looking for peace, knowing something was missing, something you couldn't identify? Did you think you needed the approval of others when it was your own approval you were chasing? You may have thought you needed any number of Earthly things when all you really needed was to realize how blessed you already are, how incredibly rich God has made you.

Peace is a state of absolute wholeness found only in God.

Peace is not merely the absence of conflict or the art of getting along with others. Peace is a state of absolute wholeness found only in God. The good news is that the God of all peace is willing to move in and live in you, yes, *you*. And when He moves in, He brings all His stuff with Him: peace, love, and joy. There's only one condition. Surrender. Absolute surrender.

Day 97: Questions for Reflection

1. On a scale of one to ten, how calm are you?
2. What detracts from your peace?
3. When have you enjoyed more tranquility?
4. What are you willing to give up for harmony?
5. What does God want for you today?
6. What deprives you of the peace Christ promised?
7. When would you like to have His peace?

AFFIRMATION 97:

I have God's peace.

Day 98:
Leaving the Past Behind

"Brethren, I do not count myself to have
apprehended; but one thing I do, forgetting
those things which are behind and reaching
forward to those things which are ahead,
I press toward the goal for the prize of the
upward call of God in Christ Jesus"
(Phil. 3:13-14).

You and I carry the past with us. Our memories make us who we are. If we couldn't remember, we wouldn't be ourselves. As we age, there are more and more memories to carry, some effervescently light, others so weighty they exhaust us. Since we can't jettison the life we've lived, what does the Apostle Paul mean when he says, "forgetting those things which are behind?"

Paul had a lot to forget. Before his conversion, he had the blood of martyrs on his hands. If he hadn't disabled those troubling memories, he probably wouldn't have traveled so extensively, founded so many churches, or written so much of the New Testament. Paul elucidated the cure for a shameful past with clarity. He allowed it to die.

"I have been crucified with Christ; it is no longer I who live, but Christ lives in me; and the life which I now live in the flesh I live by faith in the Son of God, who loved me and gave Himself for me" (Gal. 2:20).

The Bible highlights the results of painful memories in the stories of Jesus's two disciples who severely disappointed themselves. Peter, bravely wielding his sword, thought he was prepared to die defending his Lord. Yet, that very night, prideful Peter fulfilled Jesus's prophecy by denying he knew the Master three times. At the rooster's cry, Peter, ashamed of his weakness, went out and wept bitterly. Crawling out from under his pile of remorse would take time.

Judas, the group's treasurer, betrayed his Lord's whereabouts to the high priest for thirty pieces of silver. He sold the Lord of Glory for the price of a slave! Filled with sorrow at what he'd done, Judas attempted to return the money, but nothing could undo the deed. Doomed, he didn't even try to escape his mound of misery. He went out and hanged himself. Judas was right about one thing: death is the only solution to shame.

Peter agrees. "Who Himself bore our sins in His own body on the tree, that we, having died to sins, might live for righteousness—by whose stripes you were healed" (I Pet. 2:24). The outspoken disciple finally understood. Jesus had taken Peter's sins to the cross, and he could choose to consider himself dead to sin and healed—physically, mentally, and emotionally—by the stripes of the Lord Jesus Christ.

A dead man doesn't remember the past. Everything that happened before he died is wiped away, even the shame. He starts brand new. Since Peter may have been the first to discover this, Jesus instructed the women to tell the disciples *and Peter* to meet Him in Galilee. There, He reinstated the spokesman into the group and told him by what death he would glorify God.

Peter would be ready for his cross when that time came because he already considered himself dead. Thank God Peter chose the correct way to die. Where would the church be if he hadn't preached the sermon that converted 3,000 at Pentecost? What would the church look like if he hadn't broken the Jew-Gentile barrier by going to Cornelius's house to bring the Holy Spirit to the Gentiles?

The past is powerless once you stop hiding, and you stop hiding the moment you die.

Curry Blake suggests that when Satan comes to dig up your past, agree with your adversary quickly. "You're absolutely right. I did that, but that person is dead and buried. I'm hidden in Christ, so get out of here!"

Then ask yourself how important your disgrace will seem after you've been in eternity for a thousand years. If your failing won't seem important then, how important is it *now*?

Stop being afraid of the skeletons in your closet. Throw open the door; you'll be more amused than terrified. The past is powerless once you stop hiding, and you stop hiding the moment you die. So, how about it? Have you died yet? It's the only permanent solution.

Day 98: Questions for Reflection

1. How often do you think about the past?
2. Which moments bring you pleasure?
3. Which incidents are the most painful?
4. What secrets are you hiding from others?
5. How does hiding your past impact your life?
6. Who knows all your secrets?
7. What would you like to do with your past?

AFFIRMATION 98:

I leave the past behind.

Day 99:
God's Goodness

"Jesus said to him, 'You shall love the LORD
your God with all your heart, with all your soul,
and with all your mind. This is the first and great
commandment. And the second is like it. You shall
love your neighbor as yourself'" (Matt. 22:37-39).

I remember the first time I heard the saying: JOY is spelled "J" (Jesus first), "O" (Others next), and "Y" (You last). How noble! If Jesus wanted me to be last, I would try my best. So, whenever something good fell to me, I passed the treasure on to someone else. I was supposed to be last, after all, and to me, last meant last. The most ridiculous manifestation of this occurred the day I delivered my second son. When the obstetrician came to take me to the delivery room, I suggested he take the screaming woman in the next room first.

"No," he insisted. "She won't be ready for hours. You're ready now."

Don't get me wrong. I do believe in putting others first. But there has to be a balance. When I was a young mother, I thought I should make do with leftovers or nothing at all because my husband and children deserved the best. Since I wasn't working to contribute to our finances, I saved every penny I could by baking our bread, sewing our clothing, and cutting everyone's hair. I wouldn't even buy myself a pack of gum when grocery shopping. All the money was for others.

**Find time every day to enjoy
some harmless pleasure.**

One day, I asked myself: *So here you are sacrificing everything for your family. What happens next?* Following my rules, my children would grow up to sacrifice their pleasure for their children. WAIT A MINUTE! Who gets to have fun? I was working to make sure *my* children had fun, but they weren't going to qualify either. My mind leaped generations ahead to an awful realization. By my rules, no one was *ever* allowed to have guilt-free fun.

Pondering the earthshaking implications of who is actually entitled to enjoy life, I came to the amazing conclusion that God intended each of us to enjoy the things He's created! Every day, we're supposed to savor life. Enjoying actually honors our Creator. Whoa! My mental gears jammed as I attempted that paradigm shift. I felt guilty about my enjoyment!

I should have known this truth years earlier because my mother knew how to savor life. One day, when I was in tenth grade, I arrived home to find her in the kitchen with a cheesecake in her hand and mischief in her eyes. "Would you like to share this with me?" she invited. "We'll have to go into the shower in the master bedroom so the others don't catch us if they come home."

I'll never forget squeezing into the tiny enclosure with my not-so-tiny mother and relishing every creamy morsel of that sweet-tart treat. Yes, we ate the whole thing. Nobody came home while we were sneaking our snack, but the anticipation of getting caught made the experience more titillating. My mother loved cheesecake, and that day she wanted me to enjoy the dessert with her.

She also loved strawberries. One day, as I watched her eat a plate of berries, she offered me one.

"No, you eat them," I insisted. "They're your favorite."

She handed me the plumpest. "Yes, I love them, but it's more fun when someone eats with you."

So, there you have Mother's secret. Enjoy! This moment will never come again.

The Bible does admonish you and me to put the interests of others before our own. "Let nothing be done through selfish ambition or conceit, but in lowliness of mind let each esteem others better than himself" (Phil. 2:3). I don't want to leave you with the impression that selfishness is the order of the day, but I do need to ask where you usually place yourself in the pecking order.

Have you taken the top rung and ruled over the rest, or have you taken the lowest place, as Jesus admonished in Luke 14:10? Did you notice that the purpose of taking the lowest place was so the host could honor you by inviting you up higher? This is God's desire. He invites us to party with Him. He wants us to enjoy the festivities and feel honored to have been invited. Find time every day for some harmless pleasure.

Do you remember how much fun you had watching your children play? My mother sprayed a tumbleweed white and hung ornaments on it the year we couldn't afford a Christmas tree, so my brother and I could enjoy playing with our gifts around that "tree." God delights in watching His children enjoy their lives even more than Mother did. When you take time to enjoy what He's created, God smiles, so bring some joy to your Father's heart today.

Day 99: Questions for Reflection

1. Where do you usually put yourself in the pecking order?
2. In what order should you put yourself, God, and others?
3. How often do you enjoy your favorite activity?
4. How much of your day is devoted to pleasure?
5. When do you feel guilty after you've indulged yourself?
6. How do you think God feels about your enjoyment?
7. What would you like to enjoy today?

AFFIRMATION 99:

I delight in God's goodness.

Day 100:
I Love Myself

"You shall not take vengeance, nor bear any grudge against the children of your people, but you shall love your neighbor as yourself: I am the LORD" (Leviticus 19:18).

"Tell me one thing you like about yourself," my therapist challenged.

I puckered my forehead and thought until I burst into a belly laugh I couldn't stop. The question was ridiculous. A staunch perfectionist, I didn't like *anything* about myself. When I finally caught my breath, I remembered one thing I did like. "Like" is a pale word for the way I felt about this quality. I *idolized* my willpower.

"I have enough willpower to starve myself."

How little I knew. What passed for willpower was really *won't* power, a stern resistance commandeered to deprive myself of pleasure so I could rate myself as superior to others who indulged themselves. This thin reward was the only enjoyment I allowed myself. I'm amazed I survived, but I'm even more surprised at the transformation God has effected.

I don't despise myself anymore. I no longer lie awake at night trying to dream up a torture to convince me I'm still alive. I'm not afraid to venture into new relationships or admit I can't do something. I know God loves me, and He always will, no matter how badly I mess up. I've given my life to Him, and He's taken charge, leaving me free to relax. Each day is filled with new adventures, and

I enjoy them. Best of all, I no longer store up resentment against those who have wounded me. They're forgiven, every one. Even me.

So here I am, a new creation in Christ Jesus. "Old things have passed away," as Paul so eloquently states in 2 Corinthians 5:17. "Behold, all things have become new." The "all things" include my willpower. I have real willpower now, not the old won't power. I like a myriad of things about myself. I like my body. No one would call me voluptuous, yet I find being thin convenient. I even like my feet. Yes, they're bigger than the shoes in the stores, and people often step on them when they walk up to me, but they're an appreciated part of my anatomy. Why not? God gave them to me.

I like other things about myself more than the appearance of this Earthly tent. I like the fact that I've been able to forgive and even forget the pain of my past, while retaining the invaluable sense of compassion those memories generate. I like my ability to write praise and worship songs, and I enjoy my love of plants, especially the African violets blooming on my windowsill. There was a time when I didn't even know I liked flowers.

The other day, I stepped into a nursery in Flagstaff and burst into tears at the sheer beauty of the artfully arranged trees and flowers. How can people walk through such glory as though they were in a supermarket instead of a cathedral? Best of all, I like the capacity God has given me to know Him, to feel His presence among the trees and flowers He created. I love being His child, stumbling, falling, and standing again. Forever and always His.

I'm guessing you began reading this book disappointed in your inability to measure up. Some expectations may have come from friends and family, but the incapacitating ones came from you, yourself. I've mapped out a journey leading to the pinnacle of life, the summit experience you've longed for. Climb your mountain, as Moses, Elijah, and Jesus did, and God will surely meet you. When you seek the Lord with all your heart, you *will* find Him.

Light surrounds you.
Today is your day to shine.

You are a magnificent creation of the Lord God Almighty, a one-of-a-kind masterpiece. What you do with this information is up to you. You can turn the page and look at this book as one of many you've read, or you can make it your personal journey to joy. The Father's arms are open to receive you. Bring your wounded soul to Him. Light surrounds you. Today is your day to shine. "Arise, shine; For your light has come! And the glory of the LORD is risen upon you" (Isa. 60:1).

Day 100: Questions for Reflection

1. What do you like best about yourself?
2. Why does this quality please you?
3. When did you begin to like yourself?
4. Which things about yourself do you still dislike?
5. What have you gained from your pain?
6. What would you like to enjoy about yourself?
7. When do you plan to fully love yourself?

AFFIRMATION 100:

I love who I am.

Day 101:
Rock Solid

"He also brought me up out of a horrible pit, out of the miry clay, and set my feet upon a rock, and established my steps" (Ps. 40:2).

In Alcoholics Anonymous, each member introduces himself as an alcoholic, no matter how long he's been sober. Our habits wear deep ruts in our brains, but we don't have to let them control us. King David talked about being lifted out of a pit. God not only rescued him, but He also set his feet on solid ground and turned him in the right direction.

David didn't say that God filled the pit. I don't think He does. The pits *we've* dug, and even some that *others* have dug to entrap us, tend to hang around. "They have prepared a net for my steps; My soul is bowed down; They have dug a pit before me; Into the midst of it they themselves have fallen Selah" (Ps. 57:6). David is saying we can be victorious. We don't have to fall into the pit again. Wouldn't you like to know how to avoid the traps that have snagged you so often?

I asked earlier what part God plays in your recovery and what part you are expected to play. Your answer determines whether you go on your way singing in the sunlight or you fall screaming into the darkness. So, which maxim is true: "Let go and let God," or "God helps those who help themselves?" Neither is scriptural, but both contain a grain of truth.

God has provided a mighty Helper to strengthen you on your journey. You can finish strong.

Once you've been adopted into the royal family, God gives *you* the work of filling in the pits. I don't mean focusing on the past. Such a focus would only invite a tumble. I mean, focusing on Him. Every time you reinforce a godly mindset, you throw a shovelful of heavenly fill dirt into the pit. After some time, you may notice your abyss appears to be only a slight depression. Great, but this is no time for pride. Remember, a slight depression can still cause a nasty fall.

The apostle Paul writes to the church at Corinth about the need for a proactive stance. "For though we walk in the flesh, we do not war according to the flesh. For the weapons of our warfare are not carnal but mighty in God for pulling down strongholds . . . bringing every thought into captivity to the obedience of Christ" (2 Cor. 10:3-5).

Did you notice who brings every thought into captivity? You do! Your obedience to Christ is to have supreme priority. Everything else is secondary. As an active combatant in the battle for your mind, you must be willing to fight and ready to take action at the first sign of enemy activity. Numerous strongholds may still need to be cast down. The enemy erects his bulwarks the moment your thoughts stray from agreement with Christ, so post a guard at the gate of your heart.

Toward the end of Jesus's life, He said the enemy was coming but would find nothing in Him. Christ had no strongholds. Evil whispers blew right by. When Satan whispers to you, his ungodly thoughts seek lodging. Fight back. Declare the promises God has given you. They are truth.

I am a person—right now, a person with a heavenly identity. I don't need to be perfect. My Father has accepted me the way I am. He sees me as perfect in Christ Jesus. I have given Him control of my life, and I'm delighted with His workmanship. He's well able to finish the work He's begun, and I praise Him. Go God! You're awesome!

If you haven't developed a stomach for war, your spirit may be fainting. *This is exhausting. I could never keep going. I won't even start.* Those are the whispers of Satan, the accuser. Take heart! The road gets easier, and God has provided a mighty Helper to strengthen you on your journey. I'm praying for you. I know you can finish strong.

There is one particular pit, deep and entrancing, which calls with the siren song of the damned. How many times have you fallen in? The answer doesn't matter. Set your face toward God and get up one more time. You're not finished until you give up, so don't give up. Never give up. Let me say those critical words one more time. DON'T EVER GIVE UP! I don't care how bad things look. Keep going.

You're not a quitter. You have come this far because you're a victor. Snatch the first disparaging thought, and refute the lie with a Bible truth. What God says is true. What man says is questionable. What Satan says is a lie. Don't nibble on his bait. He's the ultimate scammer. Purge the old leaven, what AA calls "stinking thinking," and replace every lie with the truth of God's word.

Take the Sword of the Spirit and speak these declarations:

- I am loved. (John 3:16)
- I am important. (Ps. 139)
- I am forgiven. (1 John 2:12)
- I have been adopted by the King. (Eph. 1:5)
- God has sent His Holy Spirit to live in me and guide me. (John 16:13)
- God has provided the weapons I need to win my battles. (2 Cor. 10:4)
- When my strength wanes, the Lord strengthens me. (Isa. 40:31)
- No weapon formed against me will prosper. (Isa. 54:17)
- I can do all things through Christ. (Phil. 4:13)
- My eternal destiny is secure. (John 14:2-3)

Congratulations, pilgrim! Thank you for taking this journey with me. I'm praying you remember to keep traveling, straight ahead. I'll meet you at the tree of life in the New Jerusalem.

Day 101: Questions for Reflection

1. Which unhealthy habits trouble you?
2. How can you overcome those bad habits?
3. Where do you put toxic thoughts?
4. Which pit has God lifted you out of recently?
5. What does that pit look like today?
6. Name the strongholds you fight.
7. What do you do when the enemy knocks?

AFFIRMATION 101:

I confront ungodly thoughts immediately.

BIBLIOGRAPHY

Day 1: *An officer and a gentleman*. United States: Paramount Pictures, 1982.

Day 29: https://www.intelligence.gov/publics-daily-brief/presidents-daily-brief

Day 30: Henley, William Ernest. "Invictus." Poem. In *The Best Loved Poems of the American People*, 73-73. Garden City, New York: Doubleday & Co., Inc., 1936.

Day 30: Day, Dorothea. "My Captain." Poem. In *Best Loved Poems of the American People*, 73–74. Garden City, New York: Doubleday & Company, Inc., 1936.

Day 31: Some contents taken from Hind's Feet on High Places by Hannah Hurnard, © 1977, used by permission of Tyndale House Publishers. All rights reserved.

Day 34: Havergal, Frances Ridley. "Live Out Thy Life Within Me." Hymn. In *Enjoyingthejourney.Org/Christians-You-Should-Know-Frances-Ridley-Havergal*, n.d. https://www.enjoyingthejourney.org/christians-you-should-know-frances-ridley-havergal.

Day 34: Murray, Andrew. In *The Believer's Absolute Surrender*. Minneapolis, Minnesota: Bethany House Publishers, 1985.

Day 42: Milne, A. A. *Winnie-the-Pooh*. Methuen & Co., 1926.

Day 57: Donne, John. "No Man Is An Island." Essay. In *Meditation XVII 1624*, n.d. John Donne, No Man Is an Island, 1624 published in Meditation XVII

Day 58: "Viktor Frankl." Encyclopædia Britannica, July 16, 2025. https://www.britannica.com/biography/Viktor-Frankl.

Day 58: Applegate, Katherine. Ivan: The Remarkable Story of the Shopping Mall Gorilla. Boston, New York : Chosen Books , n.d.

Day 59: Rockafellar, Nancy. "The Story of Ishi." A History of UCSF, n.d. https://history.library.ucsf.edu/ishi.html.

Day 77: Patrick Henry, https://britannica.com>biography>Patrick-Henry

Day 62: Schulk, Jay, Paul Rozin, and Curt Richter. "Drowning Rats Psychology Experiment: Resilience and the Power of Hope." PeopleShift, n.d. people-shift.com/articles/drowning-rats-psychology-experiments.

Day 79: Trendle, George W., and George W. George. "The Lone Ranger." IMDb, n.d. https://m.imdb.com/title/tt0041038/ref_=nv_sr_srsg_4_tt_8_nm_0_in_0_q_Lone%2520Ranger%2520and%2520.

Day 80: The Discount Accident Attorneys, n.d. www.hastingsandhastings.com.

Day 81: "Lasts 10% Longer Than Duracell Power Boost." Energizer, n.d. https://energizer.com>energizer-bunny.

Day 86: *The Passion of the Christ*. United States: 2004, https://cbn.com/article/jesus/passion-christ-message-beyond-words.

Day 91: Dooley, Dennis, and Gary Engle, eds. "Superman." Encyclopedia of Cleveland History, n.d. https://case.edu/ech/articles/s/superman.

Day 91: Elizabeth, Blair. "As 'The Velveteen Rabbit' Turns 100, Its Message Continues to Resonate." NPR, n.d. https://www.npr.org/2022/04/12/1092065211/as-the-velveteen-rabbit-turns-100-its-message-continues-to-resonate.

Day 94: https://wist.info/shakespeare-william/49940/

Day 95: Abt, Samuel. "Lance Armstrong." Encyclopædia Britannica, July 10, 2025. https://www.britannica.com/biography/Lance-Armstrong.

"Gail Devers." Encyclopædia Britannica. Accessed August 7, 2025. https://www.britannica.com/biography/Gail-Devers.

Acknowledgments

I am indebted to God for giving me the 101 steps of this book thirty years ago and encouraging me to publish His wisdom now. The Sedona Christian Writers Guild, Word Weavers of Northern Arizona, and the many Christian writers' conferences I've attended all supported my efforts. My therapist provided valuable insights, but my most precious perceptions came from the wounded souls who shared their hearts with me as we journeyed together. Thank you all for being honest about your struggles. I appreciate Steve Harrison and his amazing team: Coach Cristina Smith, Editor Valerie Costa, Cover Designer Christy Day, and Coach Shannon Hazel for their support in bringing this work to print at this perfect moment.

About the Author

Eleanor Kirk is a dedicated advocate for personal transformation, bringing over two decades of experience in mentoring and healing. After overcoming a severe battle with perfectionism and the challenges of growing up as an adult child of an alcoholic, Eleanor worked with organizations like Codependents Anonymous and Alcoholics Anonymous, addressing deep-seated beliefs and fostering resilience in herself and others.

Trained as a Stephen Minister and certified Healing Rooms Technician, Eleanor has spent twenty years providing one-on-one ministry and conducting numerous inner-healing sessions, achieving profound and lasting outcomes for her clients.

Following a miraculous recovery from a five-hour brain surgery in 2024, she felt compelled to publish the book she had been inspired to write decades ago.

With a passion for education, Eleanor has taught at both high school and college levels for over thirty years, experiencing firsthand the obstacles that students face when they lack confidence in their abilities.

A retired educator from Sedona Red Rock High School, she now enjoys gardening, songwriting, and playing the guitar in her free time. Additionally, she is an avid sailor, SCUBA diver, and amateur radio operator. Eleanor holds both a Bachelor's and Master's degree from Pacific Union College.

Download the free workbook, *Perfectly Imperfect Workbook: 101 Days to a Happier, Healthier Life—God's Way* at www.eleanorkirk. com and take advantage of the section introductions, expanded questions for reflection, and lines to document your journey into a happier, healthier you.

Join the caring, support group on Eleanor's Facebook page to post your progress and questions. This is a non-judgmental gathering dedicated to your continued growth and maturity.

Watch for Eleanor Kirk's music on Amazon. She has produced two CDs of original songs combating the lies you and I have believed for too long. Each CD inspired a companion booklet with a meditation for each song as well as the scriptures that inspired them and the lies they refute. Her third CD, "Familia," is in Spanish.

www.ingramcontent.com/pod-product-compliance
Lightning Source LLC
Chambersburg PA
CBHW071453140726
47997CB00005B/1703